down they forgot

a memoir

ABBY LETTERI

children guessed (but only a few
down they forgot as up they grew ...)

– e.e. cummings

Cover photo courtesy of the author.

Cover design and formatting by JD Smith

Published by Dog's Tail Press, Wellington NZ

All enquiries to aletteri@mac.com

First published 2021
Second edition published in 2025

ISBN: 979-8-9913374-2-7 (paperback)
979-8-9913374-3-4 (ebook)
LCCN: 2021902251

For Richard

Contents

Exposures

1958–1962

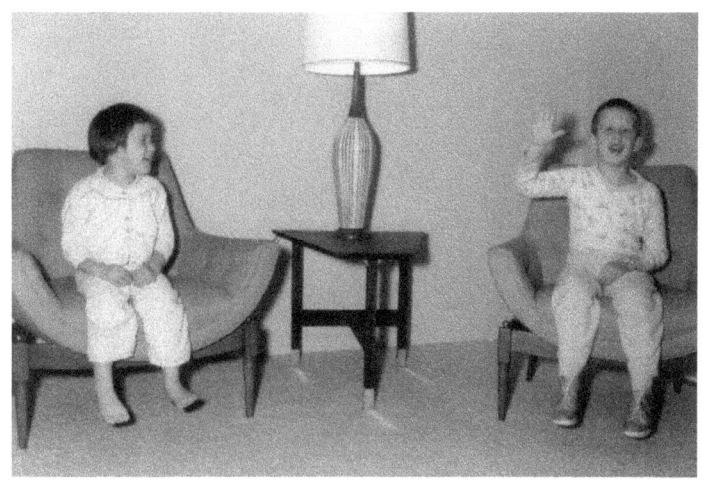

It's early morning, probably Sunday. I don't hear my dad puffing through his Royal Canadian Air Force exercises, and my brother isn't watching cartoons on TV. Maybe no one is up yet. I walk through the silent house and down the stairs, swinging slowly around the bottom banister, my free arm tracing a loose low arc. Hop off the bottom step like a bird. Hear someone moving in the kitchen at the end of the hall.

My mother is standing at the kitchen sink. Pale sun seeps through the window and stains the counter with splotches of dull light. My mother is crying. On the counter are four little glasses of orange juice, three of them empty. Later she will tell me that she poured out the last of the juice—four glasses, just enough for our breakfast—and absentmindedly drank three of them while she busied herself with other tasks.

When my mother cries, I feel culpable. I stand in the doorway flooded by the sadness that leaks from her. It fills the room and threatens to engulf me.

*

Early memories come to me with varying degrees of success, a jumble of anecdotes, snapshots, a few frames of an old movie. Nothing more. But occasionally a moment arises out of that clutter, a moment as solid and numinous as a splendid marble, lit with possibility.

*

Last night, coming home from University, I forgot to stop at the bank and didn't have enough money to pay the babysitter. Or perhaps I forgot to pick up fresh bread. A small transgression, a momentary thoughtlessness, but it's enough to cast a pall on the evening.

When I can't sleep, I tell myself stories. My daughter asks for the same. "Tell me," she'll say, as I sit with her in the dark after books have been read and the light switched off, "tell me about how I was born." So, I do.

"Now," she'll say, "tell me about how you were born."

*

A man and a small boy walk along an avenue under a canopy of spring green leaves. The boy is looking down at the tips of his brown lace-up shoes, trying to make three or four scuffling noises to every two of his father's crisply snapping steps. The boy looks up and sees two large figures sweeping towards him, clouds of black cloth swirling out around wide bodies, sinister ships with dark billowing sails gliding along the sidewalk. No legs or feet. On their heads, strange white wings flap stiffly above wide faces. Small eyes crinkled and beady. The boy pulls free of his father's grasp and cuts a wide arc though the damp grass, returning to the safety of his father's side twenty paces down the walkway that leads to the hospital steps. He looks up at his father, eyes wide as saucers.

"What was that?"

"Those were nuns," his father answers, but he's distracted. They're on their way to see the boy's new baby sister for the very first time.

*

My father was about to graduate from the Tuck School of Management at Dartmouth College. His thesis was due May 12th, so my mother stayed up late on the night of May 11th, finished typing the final manuscript and went to bed. Shortly before midnight, she woke my father: she was in labor. A neighbor was roused to look after my brother and my father drove my mother to the hospital. Expecting a long night, he returned home and was back in bed by 1 am. At 1:55 he was woken from a dead sleep by the phone. "Who is it?" he demanded.

My mother was calling from a payphone in the corridor as she was wheeled on a gurney from surgery to a bed on the ward. "Aren't you interested in your daughter?"

"I don't have a daughter," came his sleepy response. "Who *is* this?"

*

Later in the day, after visiting the maternity ward, my father and brother met cousin Jimmy, an undergraduate at Dartmouth, near the dining hall. My father scooped my brother up in his arms and balanced him on his shoulder face-to-face with Jimmy. "Dickie," my father said, flushed and eager, "tell Jimmy what happened to us today."

My brother pulled himself up and swallowed audibly. "We saw two nubs!"

*

My first memory is an over-exposed snapshot. I'm sitting on a small blanket under a newly planted tree near where the grass gives way to gravel at the edge of the road. Just a tiny nugget in the huge palm of the lawn.

I don't see my mother anywhere.

*

The yellowed edge of memory's snapshot gives way and I'm on the blanket, on the lawn. At first there's no sound, and then the hissing of the garden hose: my mother watering the lilacs. Suddenly, the ground begins to purr beneath me. I look down, reach out to the sensation, and when I look up again, I'm eclipsed by enormous silver wheels grinding through the gravel. Little pebbles are flying up and landing all around me. As the big sedan rolls off down the road, I pick up pebbles, as many as I can, and stuff them in my shining fists.

*

If I close my eyes, images ghost the inside of my lids. An icy intersection, mountains of snow tower above our car on either side of the county road. Out of nowhere, a red panel truck comes screeching and careening, an enormous crimson wall slamming sidelong into our car. We spin into a wall of snow, my father knocked senseless.

On my mother's lap in the police car, the lights and sirens of the ambulance fade away. Bright streams of blood from my mother's nose stain the furry white trim of my new winter coat.

*

I wake alone in a room, the huge face of the full moon staring in the window at me. Bars of light and shadow crisscross my body, patterned by moonlight and the slats of a crib. I don't know where my parents are or how I ended up alone in this room. All I know is that I'm in a crib. I stand up, shake the bars like an angry little prisoner and maybe I call out. A shaft of light broadens across the black floor and I look up to see a white-clad figure in the doorway.

The nurse who comes to me that night is unusually kind. When she discovers that my stuffed bear has been lost in the accident, she cobbles together a substitute from a rolled-up towel tied with the sash of her uniform, drawing on a smiling animal face with her eyebrow pencil: whiskers and eyes and a triangle for a nose.

*

It's nearly bedtime. Dickie and I are in our pajamas, pushing the chairs together. Bucket chairs: the fabric stiff and nubbly, autumn leaf orange. The pointy wooden legs catch and drag on the carpet. Pushed together, their rounded arms and scooped contours come together in a neat half-circle. We crawl up over the thick upholstered arms and into the bowl.

Dickie wobbles to his feet, reaches for the lamp and switches it off. Darkness tumbles in and I catch my breath. Down the long hall behind my back I can sense him coming. Closer and closer he moves down the hall; his shadow growing longer and more menacing with each exaggerated step. The Shadow cackles as he comes: *nyah-ah-ah.* Then silence, and suddenly Dickie grabs me into a rough embrace, our arms and legs all mixed up together in the scratchy orange bowl.

The Shadow is in the doorway. I prise my arms from Dickie's grasp and turn to see the monstrous figure looming above me. Wires sprout from the sides of his skull and disappear into his jaw. *Who knows what evil lurks in the hearts of men?* I can't help it: I scream.

From the thin opening of his barely parted lips comes the rasping finale: *nyah-ah-ah, The Shadow knows!* And Dickie and I collapse in a giggling heap.

*

After the accident, my father required two surgeries to mend his shattered jaw. The plaster skullcap cast with its wire frame became an excellent prop for playing *The Shadow Knows*, a game loosely based on an old-time radio mystery my father loved as a boy. The apparatus was painful, however, and offered only partial healing. The blow to the head he suffered on impact had another, more ominous effect. For the next several years, my father would erupt in outbursts of violent temper, which came and went without warning. He sought psychiatric help and learned to control his anger by hitting a pillow. I don't remember this, but a sketchy image of my mother floats at the edge of perception. She is blocking the kitchen door, our small dog cowering behind her.

*

My mother comes in to say goodnight. She adjusts the covers, clicks off the bedside light and leans down to kiss me. I reach up suddenly and grab her around the waist, hugging her tight. "I'm going to hold you for all and all the world and never let you go!"

Dreams

1963--1966

President Kennedy has been shot. I am in kindergarten, but they close school early and send us home. My mother is coming to meet me, and I see her a short distance ahead in the road. She is wearing a pale pink shirtdress. Her coat, hastily pulled around her shoulders, is unbuttoned even though the day is damp and raw. She is crying as she walks toward me. Tears roll down her cheeks making long grey tracks in her make-up. She wears no lipstick, or perhaps she has worn it all off by pressing her lips in grief. Suddenly the sky above us seems too large and pale, as if all color has bled away, as if we could fall up into it. As if gravity, too, might fail us. She cups her hand around my shoulder, and we walk unsteadily home.

*

Rockford is just another small town in the agricultural heartland of the Midwest, a grid of blacktop roads scored across a perfectly flat and featureless landscape. The lines of the grid form rectangular boxes; each box contains a dozen quarter-acre sections. Each section is embellished with an L-shaped single-story ranch house formed of brick and wood, with a picture window, a stone chimney and a low-slung shingle roof.

Neighbors in Rockford looked out for each other's children. In summer, screen porch doors were left open and we wandered in and out of nearly identical kitchens, always on the prowl for fresh baked cookies or cool lemonade. Our fathers went off to work in the morning, and we went off to school on foot. Our mothers baked and cleaned and drove to the market in station wagons.

One day, my mother found a big crow weaving and flopping around the back yard. Its wing was folded open and stuck up at an odd angle. 'Probably broken,' she said. We rummaged around in the garage and found the metal pen we used when our dog was a puppy and managed to trap the crow inside. Once cornered, the crow stopped banging itself around and grew quiet. My mother fed it raw hamburger and some seeds from a packet. We gave it water in the dog's bowl. She called the vet who agreed, reluctantly, to make a house call at the end of the day. Mrs. Evans, hanging out washing on the line next door, shook her head and said it'd be better just to hit it on the head and have done with it. "Just a dirty no-good crow." My mother was determined; she threw herself into rehabilitation with fervor. The vet sedated the crow and bound its wing. A few weeks later my mother unraveled what was left of the gauze, shooed the now-feisty crow with a broom into a big cardboard box and we drove it to the edge of a cornfield. We opened the lid and tipped the box on its side and watched the crow take off into the sky—shaky at first, flying low, then slowly gaining altitude as it looped the field in increasingly higher and wider circles until it was just a speck in the distance. Then it was gone.

*

After my mother's death, I received a package from Colleen, one of her few close friends. It contained a soft toy and a letter addressed to my daughter Sofia. A sticky note explained that the letter was to be saved and given to Sofia "when she is old enough to be curious." The envelope wasn't sealed, so I unfolded the letter and read it. Apart from a long description of their friendship, it gave details of my mother's life when I was a young girl and we lived not far from Colleen in Rockford. It mentioned how the two friends met in a study group focused on the United Nations. I called my dad to ask if he remembered anything about this. "A little," he said, "but you should talk to Colleen. Do you remember Colleen?"

He gave me her email address, and I sent off a quick query. The reply came within a day:

> I think it was 1963 that she showed up at my house for the first meeting of a League of Women Voters study of the UN. There was a lot of criticism of the UN in Rockford then because we had a very active right-wing group holding forth (so what else is new!). There were four of us: two rather conservative women, your mother and me. It was a very thorough and fascinating few months in which we read everything (pro and con) about the UN. The original study also got into disarmament and I know Ivanie did a lot of research into this area. She was a superb scholar, as you well know. Looking back, I'm glad we didn't all come from the same point of view. I think we all grew as a result. For people like Ivanie and me, our involvement in research and study made activists of us.

I wrote back to Colleen immediately:

> You mention your friendship. Of course, you know that during my mother's life, we moved often, and she didn't always have close friends nearby. Perhaps my mother was happiest during those years in Rockford. It makes a certain sense to me now: she was intellectually engaged on her own terms, she was active in causes that mattered to her, she had at least one good friend and she was a full-time mother which I know she loved. Both of us kids were well adjusted and healthy at that time.

I have lied a little. Thinking of Rockford as my mother's happy years has taken me by surprise. I remember my mother in turns as sad, angry and detached. Once she loaded my brother and me into the car and tried to drive away. I didn't mention any of this. Instead, I told Colleen what I recall of Rockford: what our house looked like, inside and out, how our dog herded the kittens up and down the long, narrow hallway. How I rode a two-wheel bike for the first time. It was very early in the morning and no one else was up. I took my bike out of the garage and wobbled up and down the sidewalk until I got the hang of it and the wheels went straight. Looking up to see my dad in the driveway, how proud I was to show him I could do it "all by myself." I would have been six, my daughter's age.

I remember, too, the wide, flat sky and how it seemed to span impossible distances, connecting us to the geography of an ever-expanding world. I had just started school. On summer nights the air felt cool and light. It thrummed with cricket song and, after the sun went down, the winking of fireflies. I remember my mother waking us to see an eclipse of the moon, and how I got goose bumps thinking there were Martians under the picnic table.

*

I have other conversations with my dad. I tell him how we're doing down here in New Zealand. How Joe has been on seven-day weeks and is logging in eighty to ninety hours at work. Sometimes he doesn't see Sofia for days, and she misses him. She calls his office and leaves long messages on his answering machine. He's been saving them so he can listen to her voice.

"You remember," says my dad, "I used to work those terribly long hours, just like Joe does now." I think he is saying this to comfort me. The subtext is this: *look at how well you turned out in the end. Sofia will be fine.*

I bristle, but I don't want to be unkind, so I mask my discomfort before speaking. I try for connection of another sort. I tell him I remember him coming home for dinner and then going back to work. Sometimes I'd put on my good dress and wait for him at the door. I'd have a tea party set up at my little blue table and he'd take off his jacket and sit and sip water from the little cups.

"Yes," my dad answers, "and the plant in Belvedere was miles away. It was more than an hour round trip."

In Rockford, I was so young that when my father wasn't there, I couldn't really imagine him. It was like he passed in and out of existence—more out than in. One day he called to say he was on his way home from work. This was, of course, decades before the advent of car phones. I took it literally. I thought he was calling me from the car. "Are you still there?" my dad asked. I was breathless: "Dad! I'm opening my mouth and surprising my eyes."

The Museum of Science and Industry had a tank that made thunderstorms, and a working coal mine. We stood in line for an hour or more just for a chance to ride a rattly cage to the bottom of a shaft that plunged deep below the museum floor. Donning hardhats, we climbed into little carts and trundled along on a track through a pitch-dark narrow tunnel. The ride ended abruptly in a hollowed-out cavern littered with abandoned pickaxes and lunch tins. There the Davy lamp's yellow flame would turn a dramatic blue—Methane gas!—and our guide would snuff out the wall lanterns, plunging the mine into darkness for the climax of his story: *December 24, 1932 . . . an unprecedented drop in barometric pressure . . . gas ignited by open flame lights . . . rescue teams searched in vain: all 54 miners perished that fateful Christmas Eve.*

The entire city seemed like that mine: a fabricated world of concrete and steel on multiple levels: high-rise apartments, parking lots below ground, the L train looping the city two stories in the air. Even the Chicago River was a marvel of engineering: redirected so that it flowed backwards, sludgy and docile, shifting begrudgingly away from the Lake. On St. Patrick's Day, Mayor Daley tipped his hat to the Irish immigrant voting block and dyed the river green, a thick yellow-green, the color of cartoon vomit.

Lake Michigan was big as an ocean with all the trappings. A port city on the Great Lakes trading route, Chicago hosted massive freight ships and oil tankers. Swooping gulls careened above the windy piers and great swelling waves lashed the rocky shore and froze into towering ice palaces in winter. Several man-made sandy beaches dotted the shore, protected by long concrete breakwaters we could walk out on if we dared. A long green park wrapped around the beaches and ran nearly the whole length of the shore from South Chicago to North Evanston.

*

In late summer 1965, when I was seven, we followed a moving van from Rockford to Chicago. As we drove out of town, I made up a little rhyme: *State Street, the great street—but Belvedere gets me right here!* I sang and pounded my chest and we all laughed; no one really minded leaving Rockford, least of all my dad who'd been promoted from manager of the bottle cap factory in Belvedere to a position at Corporate Headquarters. We were moving up.

By Christmas, we were settled in our first two-story house in Evanston. We were already old hands at riding the L downtown for weekend trips to the Art Institute or to a children's concert at the Symphony. These trips were never better than at Christmas, when the department stores on State Street would vie for the most captivating window displays, their success measured by the crowds of shoppers who gathered in the freezing cold to gape at the wonders of miniature mechanized worlds.

In 1965, Carson Pirie Scott's windows featured a snow-bound twilight scene with a horse-drawn carriage carrying a load of merry travellers along a track in a diminutive forest toward a tiny picture-perfect village. In the village, through brightly lit cottage windows, trees shimmered with ornaments and tables were laden with Christmas feasts. The manor house at the end of the lane was draped with boughs of fir and holly wreaths and its windows were ablaze with light. Inside, elegant dancers spun round and round in jerky circles like a dozen music box ballerinas. Across the street at Marshall Fields, Santa's workshop hummed with activity. Pixie-sized elves brandished paintbrushes and hammers to put the finishing touches on a delightful array of old-fashioned toys. There were hobbyhorses and brightly striped tops and a wooden sled with fine metal runners. Santa himself relaxed in a turn-of the-century parlor, his feet up on a stool, smoke rings rising from the bowl of his pipe. In the adjoining kitchen, one shop window over, a red-cheeked Mrs. Claus checked a tray of cookies baking in an old-fashioned cast-iron stove.

We split up and tackled the stores on our own, agreeing to meet in an hour's time under the big clock in the foyer of Marshall Fields. I had a change purse full of pocket money to buy presents for the family. A Mondrian print scarf for my mother from the museum gift shop, a laminated star chart for Dickie, and Aqua Velva shaving lotion for my dad. Too big to sit on Santa's lap, but wanting to anyway, I was relieved when my shopping was done and there were still a few coins left over for a hot chocolate in the Marshall Fields cafeteria. At the end of the day, we staggered back to the station clutching our shopping bags to catch a fast commuter train home. Fanned out across the wide granite staircase, a children's choir sang a haunting carol I'd never heard before: *So I played for him, ba-rum-pa-pum-pum*. It echoed magnificently over the heads of tired shoppers making their way to the platform doors at the far end of the cavernous hall. *Me and my drum*.

*

Evanston was a university town, which meant liberal, and shortly after we arrived, my mother joined the League of Women Voters. Nearly a decade had passed since segregation had been successfully challenged in the Supreme Court, but it was still virtually impossible for Blacks to buy or rent property in prosperous white neighborhoods—and not just in the South. My mother believed that legislation and social services could reduce, maybe even eliminate, institutional poverty. Shameful, she said, that one in three children in America lived below the poverty line. I'd seen the news-reels from Mississippi and Georgia: the ragged children with swollen bellies lined up outside dirt shacks. President Johnson had declared a war on poverty. Where would this war be fought, I wondered, and where were the soldiers? "It's a war without soldiers," my mother explained. Good people of conscience were meant to fight it, and besides, all the soldiers were going to Vietnam.

My dad used to tell a story about sharing a bedroom with his little brother, Bob. When Bob was messy and wouldn't pick up his things, my father drew a chalk line right down the middle on the floor. He didn't allow Bob or any of his clothes or toys or books to stray to his side of the line. I imagined the poverty line was like that: a great chalk mark dividing North from South. "No," said my mother. "It's here, too, right here in our community."

This, of course, was hard to see. The streets of North Evanston were lined with stately spreading oak trees. We walked to school past substantial brick houses set back on generous lots, past tidy gardens and well-maintained parks. Not a single Black family lived in our neighborhood or went to my school. "You see?" said my mother, but I couldn't, not really.

*

My mother admired Dr Martin Luther King and believed as he did in making change by working within the system, through peaceful, non-violent means. Around the country, though, patience was wearing thin and militancy was on the rise. Riot footage had become a staple of the nightly news. But my mother was not dissuaded. When Dr. King turned the focus of his movement on the issue of Open Housing in Chicago in 1966, my mother was at the ready. Dr. King stood for patience, middle-class respectability, and a measured approach to social change; my mother wore pearls to canvas the neighborhood.

*

We walk the neighborhood on a fine afternoon, knocking on doors and handing out leaflets. As we start out, we sing the old camp songs between houses: 'Dip, Dip and Glide', 'The Ash Grove' and my favorite:

Desert silvery blue beneath the pale moonlight
Coyotes yappin' lazily on the hill . . .

When a neighbor answers the door, my mother asks if she can have a few minutes of her time. The ladies wipe their hands reflexively on their aprons, touch their fingers to the permed hair at their temples. A few invite us in to sit on good couches in picture perfect living rooms, offer us something cool to drink. But our stopovers are brief. Once my mother starts to talk, the ladies fall silent. They sit on the edge of their chairs like wary animals. One says, "My husband does the voting in this house." After a few stops, we are no longer singing between houses. Now my mother falls silent. I am lagging behind when I first notice the stain blooming on the back of her carefully pressed skirt. The sight of it terrifies me. My mother rings another doorbell, and we are invited in for coffee. Mrs. Simpson leans down and takes my chin in her hand. "How old are you now, 8? You have your mother's eyes, honey," she says. I can think only of the blood leaking from the darkest part of my mother, and I don't say a thing.

Back at home my mother is angry with me. She wants to know why I didn't mention the bloodstain. "I walked this entire neighborhood with blood on my skirt? Why didn't you say something?" I sit on the wooden stool at the kitchen counter while my mother telephones every single neighbor we've visited, to apologize and offer to pay for furniture cleaning, if necessary. Her face is tight as she repeats the words again and again, and I squirm on the hard seat.

*

Most summers we took postcard vacations to places like Door County Wisconsin, where we rented an A-frame cottage near the lake or drove down to the Blue Ridge Mountains of Kentucky where black bears came right up to the car when we parked on the side of the road.

We drove for hours, sometimes all day, the road opening before us and the world disappearing in the rectangular frame of the rear window. I liked the unencumbered sensations of road trance: dotted white lines on asphalt endlessly unfolding, telephone wires loop-de-looping in the sky overhead. Sometimes I turned a single word over and over in my mind for as long as I could, for hours, until meaning unhinged itself from sound and my mind became pleasantly blank. Some days we sang as we drove with all the windows rolled down, or we played the license plate game, collecting slogans from every state in the union. Triple points for Hawaii, "the Aloha State" (the car shipped stateside on a boat!). My favorite was New Hampshire, the state of my birth, with its cryptic slogan, "Live Free or Die." I always won the license plate game because I had the sharpest eyes. One of Dickie's eyes was blind from birth and he wore thick glasses to correct the good one.

In August 1966, we drove to Sioux City, Iowa, my mother's hometown, to visit Grampa Down. Gramma Down lived at Sunrise Manor; I only vaguely remembered when she still lived at home with my Grampa in the red brick house on Perry Way.

*

I'm reading a book on the back steps and my mother and her cousin Jan are in the kitchen, baking. They're discussing my Gramma's condition. "The family illness," Jan says. I know the one: it comes from the Patterson side of the family. It took my great-great-grandfather at age forty-two, and his daughter, my great-grandmother, Jessie Patterson. She passed it to the Downs. My grandmother's sister Ruth was stricken when she was quite young, and it looks as if she's passed it to her daughter. "Shirley Ruth's got signs," my mother says, "and now mother." Jan tut-tuts and gives my mother an awkward one-armed hug. Then she leans her head out the screen door and winks at me. "Do you want to lick the spoon?"

*

My Gramma doesn't remember anybody, not even her own daughters, and she can't really talk; she moves her mouth and a kind of humming spills out. "Early onset," my mother calls it. But Gramma Down can still use her hands. When we visit, my mother pauses at the door, sucks in a breath and then sweeps breezily into the room towing my brother and me in her wake: two reluctant little sail boats, sulky and adrift.

My hair is long and straight and parted awkwardly on the side; it falls heavily over half my chubby face, which I prefer hidden anyway. Grown-ups are always pushing my hair back behind my ear. My mother is tidying the cluttered bedside table as she chats away to my Gramma's blank face. The windowsill is crammed with cards and photos and there's no place for me to sit so I hover awkwardly near the door. At some stage, my mother calls me to her side, and I'm presented. "This is Abby," my mother beams. "She's my daughter, your granddaughter." My mother is speaking loudly and clearly, bending over and patting Gramma Down's hand. "Abby's full name is the same as yours: Alice Bushnell." My Gramma stares a hole through me. Her lips are trembling as if she's trying to form words. She reaches both hands towards my head and my mother nudges me closer. "Sit down, Abby." My mother points to the hard linoleum floor in front of Gramma Down's chair and I lower myself dutifully. Floor tiles alternate in unfortunate shades of grey-white and yellow. Sunrise Manor smells of bleach and pee and it's worse down here. My Gramma's hands are on my hair. She's pulling her fingers through the snarls, gently and expertly. "She's always loved long hair," says my mother. "Pretty long hair." I don't imagine she's referring to me; I don't think of myself in terms like *pretty*. Gramma Down parts my hair and twines it slowly into two perfect French braids. It feels cool and fresh to have the hair swept off my neck on this hot afternoon. My scalp tingles and I marvel at the strength of her bony hands, working as if from some ancient blueprint.

Back at Grampa Down's house, there are dozens of perfume bottles and powder jars crowded onto the satin-skirted dressing table in Aunt Karen's bedroom. I open each one and breathe in deep draughts of the musty tinctures. This makes me light-headed, and sometimes I sneeze. Afternoons in Sioux City go on without end. There's a wire bridge high over the creek that I am not allowed to cross by myself; I'm too scared anyway. A neighbor walks her donkey up the street every morning. This year she will let me ride on it, but a motorcycle will buzz by and the startled donkey will step up the curb, stumble, and spill me onto the ground with a thud. The lawn, with its blue glass ornament distorting the sky is green, green, green, and my mother has chased all the mice and spiders from the playhouse out back. She's even fixed the little electric doorbell and the lights, and I can spend all day there if I like, reading *Black Beauty* and *20,000 Leagues Under the Sea*.

In 1966, my father left Champion to start his own company. Diversiform manufactured molded plastic inserts for packaging: cookie trays and camera box inserts and the like. The plant was on the North Side of Chicago, near Germantown. It was a cavernous place, full of huge machinery. There was a forklift truck and an old-fashioned bakery down the block where we bought little white sacks of crumbly cookies dusted with powdered sugar.

On Saturdays, my brother rode his bike all the way down to Diversiform, just for something to do. My dad was working all the time, but that was nothing new. Whenever I visited the plant, my father told the salesman, Jack, to shut his office door. Jack had a nudie pin-up calendar on the wall, which my dad didn't approve of, but he didn't make Jack take it down. With the door shut, I could still see big bare breasts though the slits of the Venetian blinds that covered the window.

Angel was the foreman. We liked him a lot. He and Dickie shared baseball stories and he always asked me about school. I told Angel I'd just finished third grade, and that my teacher, Mrs. Mayberry, had retired and given me her poster of the solar system to keep.

Dad said Angel had a family back in Mexico and he sent them money every month. One day I was sitting on the loading dock, swinging my legs over the edge. Angel came and squatted beside me. "Why doesn't your family move here?" I asked. Angel frowned and looked away. Instantly, I wished I could take it back, but then he turned and laughed and chucked me under the chin. "They are too many," he said. He took off his cap and wiped his forehead with the back of his hand. I thought he was still laughing, but then I noticed his eyes were damp. "Too many," he said again, and stood and walked away.

*

One day a man walked in the front door of Diversiform and asked for my father by name. He introduced himself as a local representative of a man who was running for city council. "The candidate is a friend of the mayor's," the man said, "if you catch my drift." He wanted to know if my father would be willing to put posters in the factory windows, endorsing the candidate. My dad politely refused.

"Politics and business don't mix," he explained at the dinner table that night. The man came back twice more, and still my dad refused. "No implicit threat," I heard him tell my mother, "but he was very persuasive. You just can't trust the Daley machine."

Lessons

1967–1970

I sit idly on the swings as the buses pull away and the playground empties of kids. I am not alone for long when three older boys emerge from the footpath that runs between the gymnasium and the playing fields. I see them in my peripheral vision, but as they enter the playground, they swing around and come up behind me. I hear loud whispers as they approach and feel the first hot sting as a piece of bark chip hits me square in the back. I sit tight and will my mother to pull up at the curb—right now. They pelt me a few times, drawing closer, calling me names that sound sharp and nasty: cracker, cunt, bitch. The bark chips sting, but they don't really hurt. I'm trying not to cry. Then a stone grazes my shoulder. I turn around in the swing, still holding fast to the chains; they are very close, just a few feet away. Big teenaged boys. One of them is smiling, but his eyes are narrow and cold. He is holding a stone the size of a golf ball, tossing and catching it. Suddenly, he whips it low and hard and it hits just below my left knee.

"What did you do that for?" I can't hold back the tears any longer. They come tumbling out with my words. I am angry and incredulous—and too afraid to turn away.

"You don't belong here, white girl," says the smiling boy. "You better get on home." He reaches down for another stone. Just at that moment, I hear a woman's voice behind me, and I swivel back around in the swing. Across the road, a Black woman wearing a cotton housedress is gesturing to me from her front porch. She has one hand on her hip.

"Come on over here, honey," she calls to me as if she were my own kin. "Come on," she calls again, and I obey. I look over my shoulder as I cross the street and see the boys looking down at their feet, walking backwards, hands jammed in their pockets, turning and vanishing behind the school.

*

In the fall of 1967, my parents volunteered me for an experimental education initiative, The Open Classroom. I was bussed into a Black neighborhood, and together with a few hundred other white kids from middle-class families, we integrated a run-down school in a tough part of town. I was nine.

In hindsight, calling it integration was a bit far-fetched. Most of the local kids were bussed out to traditional schools, while the old neighborhood school was transformed with bright paint and modern furniture and renamed the Lab School. Students in the Lab School were predominantly white, as were our teachers. Only the janitors, the lunch ladies and a handful of *promising* students were Black.

The experiments didn't stop with location or the fluidity of our classroom walls. We were placed in mixed age groupings and moved from class to class throughout the day as if we were already in high school. Our teachers, like college professors, were expert in their fields.

Lab School students participated in a variety of experiments on the effects of race, class, and teaching methodology on student attitudes and performance. During one week-long experiment, all the blue-eyed children were treated as the minority: we were not called on or chosen for special tasks, we were made to sit in back of the room and passed over for athletics. Only brown-eyed children were singled out for special treatment. A note had gone home to our parents explaining this "original teaching unit on discrimination."

On the Monday morning, I received a small blue card with a safety pin affixed to the back. I was told to take care of it, to wear it on my shirt all week and not lose it. That afternoon, I raised my hand in response to a question put to the class. My beloved English teacher passed right over me as if I were invisible, even though there were no other children volunteering answers. Later that same day I sat through the entire gym period, waiting to be called onto the tumbling mats. I never was.

On Tuesday, I forgot to wear the blue card. I was furnished with a replacement and a sharp reproach. By Wednesday, I was a blue-eyed heap of doubt and tears. I stayed home on Thursday with a stomachache. My mother kindly explained the experiment to me, but it didn't help. On Friday, the cards were collected, and the aim of the experiment revealed. I tried to admire the point they'd made, but I was ashamed of my ignorance and embarrassed at my vulnerability.

*

My first friend at Lab School was Millie Johnson. Millie was in my homeroom and during the first week we helped each other navigate the strange new terrain of classrooms without walls, independent study periods and unfamiliar faces. I was delighted to find that Millie was also in my math class. We shared, among other things, a dislike for the subject. Millie was gifted, quick, and bored. I struggled with the increasingly abstract problems, relying on Millie to check my homework and decode the intricacies of fractions and formulae.

Millie wore her hair in tight braids, smelled of talcum, and had a deep, infectious, open-mouthed laugh. We sat together in the Field House cafeteria at lunchtime. Millie knew the words to all the Motown hits on the jukebox. I fed in quarters and she punched up the songs. On rainy days, she taught me dance steps and all the hand gestures:

Stop! In the name of love
Before you break my heart . . .

When it was sunny, we raced around the packed dirt lot next to the swings, daring the boys we liked to catch us. They never did.

*

One day, Millie invited me to her house after school. I stumbled on the steps as we boarded her bus. When I lifted my eyes and looked down the aisle, I was surprised to see nothing but Black faces. Some of the kids were laughing and pointing at me, and one boy called out, "Millie! Girl, what you doin' with that white cracker on this bus?" Millie laughed, just the way she always did, but the bus driver didn't like it one bit. He stood up and told Millie and me to sit in the front seat right behind him. Then he walked slowly down the aisle to the back of the bus, glaring at the kids until they got very quiet. "Everyone's welcome on my bus," he growled. Then he returned to his seat, swung the door shut and started the engine.

*

Near the end of the term, I invited Millie to my house. It was warm and sunny, and we decided to throw a Frisbee around in the front yard. The neighbor kids, who were younger than me and usually kept to themselves, were kicking a ball around their yard. Their mother watched them from the window. When Millie and I started to play, Mrs. Hinners came out onto her front steps and called sharply to her children. Just then, their ball rolled into our yard, across the sidewalk and toward the street. Millie ran and stopped it with her foot. As she bent to pick it up, Mrs. Hinners shouted, "Don't you touch that ball!" Millie stood up slowly and backed away from the ball. One of the Hinners children darted onto our lawn and grabbed it and they all ran into the dark mouth of their doorway.

*

One night in January 1968, I'm lying on the floor reading the comics, when I catch a fragment of David Brinkley reporting from Washington: "The ten thousandth US airplane has been brought down over Vietnam." By February, I'm watching avidly along with my family, as the North Vietnamese launched the Tet offensive, and the State Department announces the highest casualty toll yet. In a single week, 543 Americans are killed in action and 2,547 are wounded. President Johnson announces he won't run for re-election.

Politics spark lots of discussion at our dinner table. Richard Nixon has declared his candidacy, and in March Bobby Kennedy finally decides to enter the race. Bobby, it seems, is the perfect choice. My parents say he'll be able to bring together Black Americans and labor, the blue-collar whites. My brother, already a political junkie, finds an old "tricky Dick" button from the 1964 Kennedy–Nixon campaign: a picture of Nixon with the words, "Would You Buy a Used Car from This Man?" But Dickie has a favorite new button, and he wears it every day: "If I Were 21, I'd Vote for Bobby."

In April, the violence hits home: Martin Luther King is shot dead in Memphis. Dickie is standing in line at Osco Drugs, waiting to pay for a couple of records, when the announcement comes over the radio. Some guy standing in line in front of him, a white man, says, "Bout time somebody got that n—." Dickie runs home red-faced and furious, angry with himself for not saying anything, for not standing up to that man. "The thing is," he says, his eyes blurring with tears, "most people who work there are Black. Some of them *must've* heard."

The night it happens, Bobby Kennedy appears on the news. He's on the campaign trail, speaking to a packed house, mostly Black people, at a union rally in Indianapolis. In the clip we can hear the agonized cries of the crowd as Bobby breaks the devastating news.

The full text of Bobby's speech is reprinted in the morning paper; my mother reads it to us at the breakfast table. Her voice breaks at the point where Bobby had quoted, *right off the top of his head*, from the Greek poet Aeschylus: "In our sleep, pain which cannot forgive falls drop by drop upon the heart until, in our own despair, against our will, comes wisdom through the awful grace of God."

*

May 8th. Four days before my tenth birthday. Dickie's got the money, but he's too embarrassed to buy the Summer Blonde himself, so he gets me to walk over to Osco with him. Just inside the automatic doors, we stop to dig around in the record bins. Dickie grabs a copy of "Susan" by a

Chicago band called The Buckinghams. "There's a cool song on the B-side," he says. We head down the hair care aisle and hang around looking at shampoo until there's no one else in sight and then we move down to the hair dye section. Dickie scans the rows of ash blondes, brunettes, and redheads until he finds the shade he wants. He says he likes the ads on TV, all those blonde kids having fun at the beach. "That one," he whispers, pointing to a box with a picture of a pretty young girl in a bikini on it. He slips me the money and goes to wait outside while I take the Summer Blonde up to the register and pay for it with my brother's five-dollar bill.

Back at home, I go out in the yard and help my mother weed the flowerbeds, creating a diversion while Dickie disappears into the bathroom with the box of dye. He's up there for a long time, and then he shuts himself in his room. "Just reading," he calls out.

At dinnertime, Dickie strolls into the dining room as if nothing's new. He's got a bright, yellow-white shock of hair spilling over his forehead; he's only dyed a streak at the front. He looks a bit like a skunk. My mother is furious, but I start giggling uncontrollably. Dickie shoots me a crooked Elvis smile.

"You can't go to school like that," she snaps. But there's nothing she can do about it. It's just going to have to wear off, which will take "weeks, maybe months," she fumes. The neighborhood kids tease Dickie too, but he doesn't care about that. He wants to see how much he can get away with at school, with his teachers. He's got a huge crush on Miss Danvers, his English teacher. On Monday, he saunters into her class. A few girls point at him and giggle, but the rest of the class passes uneventfully. When the bell rings, Miss Danvers says, "Dick, can you come and talk to me, please?" He walks slowly to her desk, the room suddenly empty and quiet. Miss Danvers starts to giggle. "Did you—did you *dye* your hair?"

My brother is crushed.

*

On June 5th, Bobby Kennedy is shot as he makes his way from the ballroom of the Ambassador Hotel to give a press conference after winning the California primary. He dies early in the morning of June 6th.

In August, during the Democratic National Convention, Chicago police take action without provocation against crowds of demonstrators. The police beat several marchers unconscious, sending dozens to emergency rooms and arresting hundreds more. Motorcycle officers ride the city streets, lashing out at anyone suspicious. On the first day of the convention, police officers club a nun and bash a group of Canadian high school students on a sightseeing trip.

By nightfall, the crowds of young protesters erupts. We watch the riot on the six o'clock news, and my brother and I exchange glances. He's been trying to explain the Yippies and their hatred for The Establishment, which includes the government and the police. On the screen, longhaired kids are screaming, "Pigs! Pigs!" at the police. Some hurl bottles and bags of human faeces. The police have riot helmets on, brandishing batons and shields. They drag a girl off-camera, clubbing at the boy who tries to stop them. I'm starting to understand. My mother switches off the TV and goes to pull a casserole from the oven. "They're trying to make change," she sighs, patting my knee as she passes my chair. "We shouldn't be in this war." But I can tell from her narrowed eyes and pinched brow that she's worried and she doesn't wholly approve.

I suppose I'm coming to think of assassinations as normal. Like body bags. I sit with my ear pressed to the cloth-covered speakers in the living room and play my 45s until they are so scratchy my mother threatens to throw them away: "Sittin' On the Dock of the Bay," "Mrs. Robinson," and Dion and the Belmonts singing "Abraham, Martin, and John"—with the new verse for Bobby. The music's a compass, a way of navigating the uncertain world. I play "Sky Pilot" over and over again:

He blesses the boys, as they stand in line
The smell of gun grease and their bayonets they shine
He's there to help them all that he can
To make them feel wanted he's a good holy man

Sky Pilot, how high can you fly?
You know you'll never, never, never reach the sky

*

King's assassination adds fuel to the fire of one of my mother's causes. After the initial blaze of race riots cools, after the Democratic Convention quits Chicago leaving the city in a stunned, uneasy silence, my mother finally agrees to let us participate in a protest march, a candlelight vigil in support of the Open Housing ordinance the League has worked so hard to get on the November ballot in Evanston. People from all over town—Blacks, whites, even the more conservative Jewish community—come out in an unparalleled show of support.

It's autumn, the blue hour. The sun has left the sky and taken the warmth with it, but the pavement beneath our feet still gives off the day's leftover heat. We've gathered on Street and are heading towards downtown Evanston, to the small triangular park near the library. My brother and I are near the front where a handful of kids hold the edges of a wide banner that spans the road: "equal rights = fair housing for all." There are hundreds of people milling around behind us, and off to the side a woman barks into a megaphone. The crowd surges up and clutching the banner, we step off. As we move down the street, a kind of orchestrated hush falls over us. My mother says this will be a peaceful demonstration, but we're not sure. We've seen the angry white mobs on the nightly news, throwing bricks at marchers. We've seen grown men and women flinch at the pop of a firecracker. We've seen the fear in their faces. We've seen their cars, smashed and burning like a garland of flame on the outskirts of Cicero.

Here, in Evanston, everything is orderly. Curious onlookers have gathered along the sidewalk to gawk as if we were a parade. Policemen in dark uniforms dot the roadside at intervals, and we pass a small assembly of television cameras and microphones. My brother grins and mugs for the cameras as we move on past. Maybe he flashes a peace sign. I turn around to look for my mother, but the crowd has swallowed her up. I move closer to my brother, feel the crush of marchers at our heels. Dickie nudges me and points obliquely with his chin to a pair of men in dark blue suits. One has a camera, the other a notebook and pen. They might be journalists, but they're standing clear of the march and their faces are set and expressionless. "FBI," whispers my brother, "or maybe the Red Squad. Mrs. Cohen told me. They're keeping tabs." The notorious Red Squad of the Chicago police are known to hang around rallies and demonstrations, he says, taking notes and photos, working up dossiers on agitators. Later, when we tell my mother she'll pooh-pooh the notion, but I've seen them with my own eyes, and I know it's true: it's us and them. It's dawned on me that the police are not always our friends.

We come to the park across from the library as the last light drains from the sky. The marchers fan out around a low platform where speeches will be made. Candles flicker on and throughout the crowd earnest faces are suddenly lit from underneath—like Halloween, great fun for us. We set the banner along the front of the platform just as my mother materializes from the crowd. She pulls a couple of stubby white candles from her purse and hands one to each of us. The ends are jammed into little flowers of foil to keep melting wax from dripping onto our skin. On stage, a woman in a long dress plays guitar and sings, "We Shall Overcome."

In November, voters in Evanston pass a tough, enforceable open housing ordinance into local law. It is the first of its kind in the nation.

*

On December 21, Apollo 8 is launched. It's the first manned mission to the moon. On Christmas Eve, we gather in the living room, transfixed by televised footage of the milky lunar landscape and the crackling voice of astronaut Jim Lovell, saying: "The vast loneliness is awe-inspiring, and it makes you realize just what you have back there on Earth." Then the crew takes turns reading from the book of Genesis.

At the end of the broadcast, Frank Borman adds, "And from the crew of Apollo 8, we close with good night, good luck, a Merry Christmas, and God bless all of you—all of you on the good Earth."

*

The Unitarian Fellowship in Evanston had a reputation for social justice and peace activism, and my mother, eager to meet like-minded people, signed us all up. Towards the end of 1968, she volunteered to teach the fifth grade Sunday school class, and for the first time ever my brother and I attended classes too.

The fourth grade curriculum placed special emphasis on creation stories from around the world. I remember vividly a story from Mexico: Mother Sun and Mother Moon, two sisters who carried baskets down to the cooling earth. They sprinkled seeds and pebbles and watched mountains and rivers appear. All manner of creature sprung from the bones they tossed. "Blood and memory connect all living things," the teacher told us, "even to this day."

These fanciful myths were balanced by scientific explanations of the origins of the planet and our species. One day, the teacher brought in an electric frying pan and cooked up a batch of butterscotch pudding until it developed a thick, hard crust. She switched off the heat, and we gathered round as the surface cooled and cracked just as the earth may have done all those millions of years ago. I thought of the two sisters sprinkling their seeds and bones while the teacher handed out plastic spoons and we gobbled up the evidence.

Every few weeks, we drove off in a bus to attend services at other people's houses of worship. We endured mass at a gloomy Russian Orthodox Church. Reeling and heady with thick incense, we bobbed up and down with the congregation and wondered what was being said. At the synagogue down the road, we had to cover our heads and bow while the cantor droned on in a sonorous baritone. No one ever explained what was going on. But at the magnificent Baha'i Temple in suburban Winnetka, we were told that the lacy, nine-sided dome towering above us was meant to show that we could make the world sacred through acts of human devotion. The sparkling blue-and-gold interior filled me with joy, but I noticed there were no people worshipping here, just tourists with cameras and our rag-tag group of noisy kids.

Towards the end of the year, I had a spiritual crisis. I cried in my mother's arms and begged not to go back to Sunday school. "I know what everybody else believes," I said, "but I don't know what I'm supposed to believe." I wanted a simple answer to clear it all up. I asked my mother, "What do we believe in?" and when she didn't respond, I switched to a more urgent plea: "What do *you* believe?"

Eventually I coaxed an answer out of her. She didn't believe in divinity, but in a kind of unifying force or principle. She took it, she said, from years of scientific study. "Look closely at the inner working of a plant, or the human body," she explained. "Look at the stars." I was incredulous; science and the gobbledy-gook of religion seemed diametrically opposed. "There's a pattern at the core of life, not so much a divine plan as an intricate blueprint. And then there's human aspiration.

"Some days," she said, "I sense it as a movement towards good." My mother didn't believe in God—there wasn't going to be a quick fix—but I understood that she couldn't bear to be without belief.

"There's evidence for optimism everywhere you look," she added, lighting a cigarette and falling silent.

*

I understood little of my parents' troubles. For over a year, Diversiform had been on the skids. Orders dried up and the expensive machines sat idle. My dad was forced to let go all but a skeleton crew. Jack left, but Angel stayed on and my dad struggled to pay him.

It'd been months since we lit a fire on a Sunday evening, sat around the living room eating popcorn and apples and reading aloud from our favorites: Robert Frost's "After Apple Picking" or Whittier's "Snowbound", which my dad could recite by memory. We didn't bother with our favorite Sunday programs, *The Walt Disney Family Hour* or *Wild Kingdom*. Even politics began to take a back seat to the immediacy of our predicament.

One night at dinner, my parents' icy conversation erupted into a genuine argument. Before I realized what was happening, my mother whipped a fork at my father, grazing his temple. We froze, watching in horror as my father stood and lifted his end of the table with both hands, dumping all the plates and loaded serving dishes into my mother's lap. A frozen moment, and then my mother sucked in air and started yelling. In our family, voices were rarely raised; my brother and I had never heard anything like it. We bolted from the room and scrambled up the stairs. On the landing, Dickie hissed, "We've got to call the police. They're going to kill each other." We ducked into my parents' bedroom and Dickie grabbed the receiver of the phone on the bedside table. His hands were shaking, his face gone white. Just as he began to dial, my mother rushed in and put her finger firmly on the receiver. "Who are you calling?" she demanded.

Dickie and I spoke at once: "Nobody," he said. But I cried out, "The police!"

My mother sat down on the edge of the bed and gathered us into her arms. "It's alright," she said, soothingly, but the muscles in her neck were tense. She was clenching her teeth. "There's no need to call anyone." My brother broke away and ran to his room; my mother let him go. "Come on," she said to me. "Let's get you to bed." It was a full hour before my bedtime, but for once I didn't protest.

*

The failure of my father's business slowly unravelled us. We sold our two-story house in North Evanston and moved into a duplex near the university. It was a respectable address, but less so. Our bedrooms were small, the hallway narrow and dark. My mother was constantly reminding us to tread lightly on the stairs and keep our music down. Not easy, when music increasingly dominated our lives. The idea that we didn't own the place, and that we'd lost our house and all our savings, never entered my awareness.

New rituals governed my parents' days, their concerns turned inward on survival. My mother returned to work. Recruited by a neighbor who had served with her on a League of Women Voters committee, and with no prior experience, she took a grant writing position in the development office of Northwestern University. Her learning curve must've been steep, and the adjustment fraught with difficulty. I don't remember this. I only remember coming home after school to an empty apartment that wasn't quite like home.

*

On July 21, 1969, the day after Neil Armstrong took his first steps on the surface of the Moon, my brother had his first psychotic episode. He was fourteen.

We were on our way to visit my grandfather in Sioux City when it happened. My dad had a new job at a Chemical company and couldn't get away, so my mother drove us out on her own. We had to leave very early—at the crack of dawn—to make the twelve-hour trip in a single day. My brother had never been a morning person, so we didn't notice anything wrong until we pulled into the Howard Johnson's in Davenport for lunch. My brother sat up and whispered tensely that he wasn't going "in there." My mother argued with him, but Dick, pale and shaking, was too scared to move. My mother had been driving for several hours already, and she'd had enough. "Fine," she said. "You stay here." She parked near the front door and chose a booth where she could keep an eye on the car, and we ate in awkward silence.

How we got from the restaurant to my grandfather's house three hundred miles to the West, and how we got home again, I don't quite remember. Somewhere West of Iowa City, the water pump on the old Skylark blew. By the time the tow truck pulled into a gas station just off the highway, it was too late in the day to send for replacement parts. I sat up all night with the drone of florescent lights drilling into my ears, drinking flat Coke from a paper cup. My mother bought a pack of cigarettes and smoked each one right down to the filter. Only my brother slept, writhing and fitful on the back seat of the wounded car.

Grampa Down said Dick had the flu and he gave him something to help him rest. My brother remained agitated and withdrawn, holed up in Gramp's bedroom in front of the color TV. He told me he thought the food might be poisoned. Every night he wrapped his meat in a paper napkin, snuck it from the dinner table and threw it away.

*

The following year, we took a family vacation to see the Indian burial mounds in Wisconsin. On the first day out, we stopped at a rest area just off the highway where there were picnic tables and a few ragged trees for shade. My mother was busy setting out the packed lunch: cheese sandwiches, carrot sticks, and some fruit. Dickie refused to get out of the car. After a while, I wandered over and offered him some tepid lemonade. He crouched like a scared dog in the back seat and asked me, "Did you drink this stuff?" He was shaking.

A semi pulled off the interstate, grinding down its gears as it coasted into the wide trucker's lot on the far side of the public toilets. Dickie flew into a panic, yelling at my mother, "We've got to go! We've got to get out of here!" He stabbed the air with his finger in the direction of the truck.

We had to cut the vacation short. Everywhere we went, Dickie imagined that people were out to get us. The entire world had assumed a malevolent nature. I spent a lot of time in the back seat, trying to calm him down and reassure him. *No, that man near the public toilets doesn't have a gun. Dad's fine, he's not driving too fast.* But my brother refused to go anywhere, and we couldn't just leave him in the car.

Back in Evanston, my parents sought family counselling. We went to one session, and at the end the counsellor told us we were fine as a family and didn't need therapy. He said our center of strength was my father and we just needed to follow his lead. A few weeks later, when my brother had settled down and was a little less withdrawn, he told me he'd walked out of that counsellor's office with a hollow feeling, confused but knowing we'd been touched by a bullshit artist. I had no idea what he meant.

Crimes

1971–1973

My brother, nearly sixteen, doesn't want to be called Dickie anymore. He tries Frank for a while, his given name, but this is nearly impossible for us to manage, so he settles for Dick. We're sitting front and center at Amazing Grace on the Northwestern campus. It's Sunday afternoon, and we're drinking 7-Up and singing along to John Prine. He's no big deal, just a singer-songwriter on the coffee house circuit, but we've heard a few of his songs and we know all the words:

Cuz' your flag decal won't get you into heaven anymore
it's already overcrowded from your dirty little war . . .

Between sets, I'm hoping that John Prine will come over and sit with us. I tell Dick he's the man I want to marry. Dick says, "You're a kid, and besides, he's already married." I don't care.

My brother is telling me about what happened two years ago when my dad's business failed. He says, "When the mob tried to infiltrate the company, Dad resisted. They wanted a controlling share in exchange for 'deals' on supplies and stuff." I don't know what this means. "You know," he says, "the stuff Dad had to buy to make those plastic inserts. Raw plastic, I guess. These guys, the mob, were offering 'protection'. But Dad went to the police, and the police sent him to the FBI. He had to go downtown and look at page after page of mug shots. He saw two of the men that had been visiting him at the plant."

"So, what happened?"

"It wasn't long before Dad's suppliers stopped calling

51

back, and the prices of the stuff he needed to buy skyrocket-ed. Some things he really needed he just couldn't get. Out of stock, they told him. Then Mom started getting the phone calls."

My brother is leaning over the table and his eyes are really wild. I look around to see who is watching us, how far we are from the door. He keeps talking, but he gets quieter.

"They threatened to kill us," he says.

*

When my dad's business failed, I was ten. By the time I started to piece together what had happened, I was nearly a teenager. I wore a key on a string around my neck, but I kept losing it and my mother would have to leave work early to come home and let me in. One day, I arrived home alone. I didn't have the key and the phone was ringing. I could hear it through the thin pane of glass on the back-porch door. I knew it was my mother calling and that she would be wor-ried if I didn't answer. I made a fist, and without thinking I punched through the glass and reached down to unlock the door. I picked up the phone with blood running down my wrist, sank to the floor and cried, "I think you'd better come home, mom. I'm bleeding all over the place."

*

My first partner in crime was a leggy redhead, the taller half of a set of twins. Marie had an exotic quality that tran-scended even her status as a twin. She was as singular and glamorous as a thirteen-year-old could possibly be.

I met her sister Sylvie first, in social studies class. We

gossiped together in the back row about our teacher's obsession with military technology and torture. We were studying the Middle Ages or, more precisely, we were subjected to daily accounts of the effects of the Iron Maiden and other popular medieval torture devices. Slipping notes back and forth, we discovered our mutual love of horses. Sylvie and Marie were about to start lessons at a riding stable in the Forest Preserve out past Skokie. At the end of our first week of shared confidences, I invited Sylvie for a sleep-over and she replied, "Oh! Me and Marie? Yeah, we'd love to."

I fretted all day about breaking it to my mother that we were having two overnight guests, but she didn't blink. She was anxious for me to get along socially at school. Secretly, I was terrified of Marie. She possessed all the qualities I lacked: confidence, attitude, beauty, and breasts.

Sylvie bore an uncanny resemblance to the half-naked girl-child on the Blind Faith album cover with a mop of strawberry curls, small, pale breasts, and a pouting mouth. She kept a journal in a quad-lined French notebook, had an infectious laugh, wrote poetry and smoked. Marie was a breath-taking doppelganger for Botticelli's *The Birth of Venus*. Her copper hair was long and wispy at the ends; it appeared wind-whipped and elegant at the same time. She had a long Italianate nose, bow-shaped lips, and a chiselled jaw and chin. She was loose and long-limbed and comfortable in her body. It was amusing—and unsettling—to see our male teachers stutter when they addressed her; boys went quiet in her presence. Marie alone seemed untroubled by the turmoil of pubescence: she wore a permanent half-smile that hovered between disdain and wry amusement. I thought of her as a wild creature, more unicorn than horse.

*

Sylvie and Marie turned up on Saturday afternoon with their toothbrushes and pajamas in a paper shopping bag. Their mother was French—Sylvie had warned me. Lorraine smoked unfiltered cigarettes and spoke with a heavy accent, slurring her rs like a drunk. Her hair was so blonde it was almost white, cropped unfashionably short. It looked like she cut it herself with kitchen scissors. "Maman is out of control," Sylvie whispered conspiratorially. "Last weekend she picked on my father until he got so mad, he threw the vacuum cleaner down the stairs. It smashed to bits."

They walked all the way to our apartment on Prairie Avenue, with Lorraine pushing her old, black one-speed bike. My mother and Lorraine spoke for a few minutes out on the sidewalk, and I winced when I heard my mother's shrill mispronunciation of Lorraine's breathy name, 'Well, Lur-AYNE. Delighted to meet you.' As Lorraine got on her bike, I noticed her unshaven legs beneath a home-made skirt. The calves were strong and shapely, and as she curled the tips of her soft cloth shoes around the pedals and struck off purposefully, her legs looked for all the world like the arms of a circus acrobat bicycling away upside-down. I was dizzy with the foreignness of it. I stood and waved like a goofy little kid as Lorraine disappeared up the street. Sylvie and Marie had long since turned their backs on their mother and were halfway up the path to our door.

*

The evening didn't go as planned. Sylvie got a headache and went off to sleep in my room before eight o'clock. My mother helped Marie and me fix up beds in the family room and let us stay up as late as we wanted. After my parents went to bed, we snuck into the dining room and stole two juice glasses of Scotch from the decanter. Marie filled the bottle back up to the top with water from the kitchen tap. It was my first drink. I gulped down the stinging liquid and giggled as my head began to spin. We lit a candle on the coffee table between our makeshift beds and got under the covers. I was excited, watching the shadow light loom large and dance above us. Marie was cool and still, but talkative.

"Oh, yeah. I kissed Evan in the back of the music shop," Marie told me. Evan was my new guitar teacher. Marie and Sylvie had been taking lessons for months. Evan looked a bit like Arlo Guthrie, and I had a painful crush on him. I made up excuses to walk past the music shop on the way home from school, peering in and running away if he spotted me and waved. I didn't begrudge Marie the kiss; I just wanted details. "He tasted leathery," she said. "Not like Del. He tastes like vanilla custard." I tried to imagine tasting someone's mouth. I had only kissed my pillow.

"I'd go all the way with him," she mused.

"But Del's old—I mean, he's nearly college age," I said. I wasn't sure I knew exactly what she meant, *all the way*, but I was impressed.

"Seventeen," Marie corrected. She rolled onto her back and snorted. "He's got hash, the real stuff. We should go over there tomorrow. Besides," Marie rolled over and pinned me with a look, "he's got a cute little brother, a real freak."

I'd heard you couldn't get high the first few times you smoked, and I said as much. Marie snorted again, but not unkindly. "No, this stuff will get you fucked up right away."

*

In August, we moved to another second-floor apartment, on Judson Avenue in South Evanston. The day we moved in, I was thrilled to look down the block and recognize the Andersens' rambling three-story white frame house. Sylvie and Marie were my neighbours!

Two professional couples lived in the back wing of our new apartment building, upstairs and down. We were in the top front apartment, and a dignified old woman named Mary lived downstairs. Mary was a retired schoolteacher and took an immediate interest in us. We were the only family with children in the building. Sometimes, after school, as I pushed open the heavy glass door that led from the entryway to the stairs, Mary would open her front door and call to me, offering a snack. Mary was nice enough, and I liked the cookies she kept on hand, but talking to her wasn't easy. Her questions ("How do you like your classes?" or "What are you reading in English?") were quickly exhausted, and it never occurred to me to make conversation by asking her anything in return. I scarfed down the cookies and made excuses about homework so I wouldn't have to linger. Truth was, I didn't care if I did my homework or not. If I had to do it, I slapped it together in the morning during homeroom. I suffered through French classes red-faced and stuttering, forced to answer questions I rarely understood. But shame didn't motivate study. I scraped by all year with as little effort as possible.

My brother was more remote than ever, holed up in his darkened room after school, scribbling in notebooks or sleeping. I started spending more and more time with Marie and Sylvie. Their parents were professors at Northwestern. They worked odd hours and were often home, holed up in their respective offices, and they let us come and go as we pleased. Marie and Sylvie shared a bedroom in the attic, where we could play music as loud as we liked and smoke— cigarettes and pot—out of the closet window. We prowled the neighborhood at our leisure, shopping for whimsical outfits at the Salvation Army, dropping into Hear Here Records or the head shop where we bought rolling papers and little hash pipes and incense to mask the evidence. I became a regular fixture at the Andersens' dinner table.

Sylvie and Marie were always reading, and I tried to keep up. Marie has just finished *The Chronicles of Narnia* for the second time, but I felt lost in the complicated fantasy world. It was Sylvie who loaned me her copy of *Tess of the D'Urbervilles*. I was thrilled by the breathless drama of Tess's star-crossed life and crushed at her demise. I'd never fallen so hard for a novel. I took away from Tess a small scrap of comfort: her steadfast belief in "the religion of loving kindness," which sustained her in the absence of any other spiritual belief.

I copied everything that Sylvie and Marie did. Sylvie wrote in a journal, so I did, too. Marie was making great progress on the guitar, so I struggled to develop my calluses and finger-picking techniques. Marie mastered open tunings, and I plucked out *Needle and the Damage Done*, which I played over and over while Sylvie and Marie sang harmony. Sylvie loved old movies, so one day we all skipped school so we could watch a youngish Marlon Brando in *Mutiny on the Bounty* on the afternoon movie. Cigarettes were easy to come by; Lorraine bought them by the carton and left them lying all around the house. We smoked and talked and listened to music, and the dark unsettled atmosphere at home faded in importance.

*

Marie liked to steal, and soon I was her willing accomplice. She was a petty thief: she didn't go in for the big-ticket items like records and clothing. The end product wasn't important. Her motivation was amusement, the thrill of the game.

Our favorite haunts were the big variety shops downtown. We would come away from an afternoon's work with Marie's shoulder bag stuffed full of lipsticks, hair accessories, pens, paperclips, and matinee boxes of chocolates and licorice. As often as not we would dump the entire day's harvest in an alley on the way home. We imagined other children, perhaps poor children, stumbling on one of our caches and delighting in all the little plastic objects and pretty things.

Marie put me to work as her foil. She gave me pocket money, and we stood around the display racks trying to decide which color hair clip to buy, or which pen. While I deliberated, Marie stuffed her bag. And when I finally made my selection and took it to the checkout counter, my meager purchase gave our presence in the shop an air of blamelessness. We were invincible.

*

When we get caught, it goes like this.

We duck into a store we don't usually frequent because Marie needs a notebook for school and she's just remembered. Our bags are stuffed full of bounty from the other shops we've raided and we're in a bit of a hurry. Marie gets careless. I'm hanging around, flipping through the 45s, while she goes for the notebook and a pen without deliberation. Get in and get out quick. Or something like that.

As we walk toward the automatic doors, I feel a hand on my collar. Turning around, we're face to face with a little bulldog of a man looking like he's about to explode. He grabs Marie by the arm and marches us to the back of the store, through a swinging door and into a dim corridor. "Just what do you think you're doing?" He is focused on Marie. I may as well not be here. "You punk kids, trying to rip me off!" Marie doesn't answer, so he grabs her long braid and slams her against a metal cabinet. He is red-faced and there's spit spraying from his mouth. "*Just what do you think, huh? What?*" A young clerk pushes through the door in a burst of light. Behind him, a gaggle of shoppers are gaping at us. We're the freak show, the entertainment. The bulldog stops barking and lets Marie go. "You deal with it then," he growls, flexing a fist and stabbing the air with an angry finger. And then he stomps off.

The clerk's name is Dave. He tells us he's the assistant store manager and asks if he can look in our bags. My breath catches in my throat and no words come, but Marie is as cool as ever. Tucking a loose lock of hair behind her ear, she says, "No, you can't. But, here." She pulls the notebook and pen out of her bag and hands them over. "That's all I took," she says. "I needed them for school."

Dave takes our names and tells us to sit down while he makes a phone call. Then he walks us back to the front of the store. I shift from foot to foot and try to ignore the rubber-necking shoppers, but Marie stands stock still, eyes narrowed, lips firmly pressed. Dave tries to make small talk, asks about school and when we don't answer, he shrugs and says, "You won't be able to come in here anymore, ok? Like, not even to shop, you know?" He sounds a bit sad about this, and I'm not surprised that he's looking only at Marie. *I may as well not be here.*

The automatic doors rattle open and a man strolls in. He's got a big mustache and he's wearing bell-bottom jeans, just a little too short to be cool, and a corduroy jacket. The doors hiss to a close behind him. Dave and the man shake hands. "Plain-clothes," Marie whispers. It takes a minute to register her meaning. The man is looking us over. He folds his arms in front of his chest, arranges his face and lifts an eyebrow. "I'm Officer Gunstone, Evanston PD," he says. Marie says, "Duh." I don't think she actually says it, but I know she's thinking it and I'm scared as hell she's going to say it out loud, so I nod quickly, whisper "Yes sir" and look at my shoes. Officer Gunstone asks each of us our name, address and phone number and writes it all down in a little notebook. He asks our parents' names and our father's occupations. Marie says both her parents are professors at the University and he ignores this. Writes a few more lines then slips the notebook into his breast pocket.

Officer Gunstone says he's going to take us home and turns to the door, but Dave stops him. Dave says, "You smoke a pipe, don't you Phil?" Officer Gunstone tilts his head and lifts an eyebrow again. I hear Marie's voice in my head: *his signature move*. We're standing next to a rack of tobacco pouches. Dave waves his hand and says, "Help yourself." Officer Gunstone selects a pouch and slips it inside his jacket. "Take it easy, won't you?" Dave says. It's more question than salutation.

We're in the back of a plain brown sedan and my stomach is turning cartwheels. Marie is clutching her bag in front of her chest. Neither of us is talking. Dionne Warwick is on the radio singing "Walk On By" but all the police gear is there, too, hidden below the dashboard. The dispatch radio crackles to life and spits out random words: "Oh-5 on Dempster, headed West."

A block before Marie's house, Officer Gunstone pulls over and tells us to get out. "Go home," he says, "and be cool. Wouldn't want to frighten your parents, seeing you get out of a strange man's car."

We climb out and start walking slowly as if we have lead weights in our shoes. Officer Gunstone toots the horn and we turn to look. He rips the page from his notebook, holds it out the window and tears it into shreds. They fall from his fingers like tiny blossoms.

*

It's a game I play underwater. I hold my breath, close my eyes and plug my fingers in my ears in order to block off all but the most bodily sensations. Then I lie still as long as I can, willing the thing that isn't my body to pull away like something rubber until it floats far beyond the boundaries of my skin, until the connection to my physical body dissolves. Unencumbered, I look lightly back at the diminishing world. In the cold waters of the pool, my body drops away, and that other animal, the clear-seeing eye, soars upwards into colorless space.

*

Summer. Joanne's wedding. Drinking vodka on the diving board of Gramp's pool. Hanging out on the roof of Nan's VW at the drive-in theatre, we listen to the soundtrack of *The Russians Are Coming* while we watch a biker flick on the opposite screen. *The Born Losers*. A pretty girl is shot between the eyes. When nothing works to curl my hair, Joanne cries because I won't look like all the other bridesmaids.

Nighttime, and the wedding party is booming and blathering. Everybody's drunk. My mother's gone to bed, and one of the groomsmen corners me in the back garden, kisses me and feels me up. I don't like the man, but I like the sensation of big hands on my chunky girl-body, on the little mounds of my breasts. I run away like a good girl and later one of the uncles brings me a beer. Everybody's been sneaking me drinks and I'm pretty gone. The music has stopped, and people are talking into the microphone under the big tent. We wander over and it's time to throw the garter, the bouquet. Everyone is jostling and pushing and laughing and I'm shoved right to the front of the herd that crowds around Jo. The blood red garter slides off her tanned thigh and sails above my head. The bouquet lands in my arms and everybody laughs hysterically. I laugh, too. I flip my impossibly straight hair and toss the bouquet to someone else.

*

One weekend, my mother called a family meeting. She sat us down and explained our budget in great detail. We had exactly ninety-one dollars a week to spend on food and gas for the car. Seven dollars a week for each of us kids for bus fares and lunch money. My mother's train fare was nearly twice that. One-hundred-seventy dollars a year each for clothes ("This includes your winter coat and boots, Abby— you're at least a size bigger. You're going to need new ones"). Another forty-two dollars each for school supplies and books. We were meant to come away from the exercise with a sense of camaraderie, of pitching in and managing it all together. My brother was hunched over the table, characteristically cupping his hand around his bad eye and squinting in the light. Grey hair was sprouting at my mother's temples and in the part of her blunt-cut hair. My dad had grown long sideburns and bought a pair of striped bell-bottoms that were way too short. He wore them, embarrassingly, with a white belt and shoes. I wondered what he was trying to prove. Even the dog had developed a skin condition and had been shaved. He looked like some kind of pathetic Dr.

Seuss creature, scrawny with an enormous plume for a tail. And I was chubby and sullen. A pretty sorry bunch.

My mother remained cautious but hands-off about leaving me alone while she worked. Money was too tight for anything extra, like drama classes, and I was too old for a sitter. Nights, my mother slumped at the dining room table, worrying over piles of work she brought home from the office. She clicked away at the big buttons of my dad's old adding machine, calculating sums on a long paper tape. She pulled out the old manual typewriter. It had an oily machine smell and keys that gave way and sprang back under my fingers with satisfying resistance. Afternoons, when there was nothing to do and my brother was sleeping, I pecked around the keys and typed out my poems. The keys gave way, and the bars flew up and hit the paper, *thwack thwack*. My mother said she worked in development; but I had no idea what that meant, and I never asked. She looked unhappy. That was all I needed to know.

*

The tiny dining room was packed with furniture: the piano and the teacart on one wall, the china cabinet squeezed in next to the kitchen door. There was barely room to pull out the chairs on both sides of the table. The piano sat silent now except for rare weekends when, in an effort to bring us together, my mother pulled out the bench after dinner and played a few old Beatles songs. We gathered round, more or less reluctantly, and joined her pure soprano with our wobbly voices, trying to hit her notes:

One day you'll look to see I've gone.
For tomorrow may rain, so I'll follow the sun.

My brother always retreated to his room at the first

opportunity. He wasn't doing very well. He'd had his wisdom teeth out and the pain medicine seemed to make him worse. He slept all the time and some nights my dad slept in his bedroom on a foldout cot because of his "condition." Sometimes I'd knock on his door and he'd let me come in and listen to music with him: Dylan and Hendrix and Neil Young. One afternoon, my brother copied out a long passage from Dylan Thomas, which he wrote, first in pencil, on his wall. I helped him trace over the words with dark acrylic paints. I came home the following day and he'd drawn a big distorted face in a kind of swirl of purplish clouds around the words. A self-portrait. I imagined my mother would be really pissed but she went flat when she saw it, sighed, and said we could always paint over it when we leave. "It'll take several coats of paint to cover that," said my dad, but he didn't seem angry either. I couldn't believe my brother was getting away with it. Eggshells at our house.

*

When my parents aren't flat, they're fighting. Up in the front of the apartment, in their bedroom, they argue mostly about money. My dad borrowed tens of thousands of dollars from friends when he set up Diversiform. He tells my mother he's going to pay it all back, *every last cent*. I can't understand why they're so angry and my stomach is wound in a tight coil. I lie on my side to relieve the pressure, and the more I lie there, the more resentful I become. I tell Sylvie and Marie that my parents are ruining my life. I keep a notebook under the bed that Sylvie's given me, quad ruled with a black plastic cover and French writing on the flyleaf. Sylvie's penned an inscription to me on the first page, something from May Sarton about daring to be myself, "however frightening or strange that self may prove to be." I'm filling the notebook with my deepest and most alarming thoughts.

Meanwhile, I'm getting into trouble, and nobody notices. I've learned to forge my mother's signature so that I can ditch school and write my own excuse notes. Junior high is boring and traditional. Quite different from free-form Lab School, it's buttoned-down and laced-up tight. I hate everything I have to learn by rote: French, math, the periodic table of the elements. Even English sucks because I have to diagram sentences and analyze the parts of speech. This feels like unnecessary surgery, performed without anaesthetic. I'm off at lunch period behind the sports shed at the back of the playing field, sniffing cooking spray from a plastic bag, trying to walk immediately afterwards and falling down laughing. Del's little brother Eli is in my grade. He's a freak with hair down past his shoulders, nearly as long as mine, and he wears an Army jacket with a small frayed hole in the shoulder ("bullet hole" he says). Eli's got fuzz growing above his lip and he walks me partway home from school most days. We smoke joints up on the L tracks and he tells me he's got blotter acid at home. Do I wanna trip? Yeah, I say. So, he's my boyfriend now; we even hold hands.

One day after school, we blow a joint on the tracks and grab the bus up to Del's place on Chicago Avenue near Dempster. We go to Baskin Robbins first, and I order my favorite: a chocolate mint hot fudge sundae, no nuts, no cherry. I'm in the habit of saving my lunch money for this. At Del's, a bunch of freaks are sitting around smoking hash from a water pipe. Eli and I each take a hit and then he leads me off to Del's bedroom. The walls are rippling like canvas in the wind. The naked bulb suspended from the ceiling is a weak and distant sun. Eli wiggles out of his clothes and I laugh to I see him standing there, limp and white with his fantastic head of black curls. I'm wearing a granny dress with loose elastic, so it comes off easily and suddenly I'm standing there in my panties, my face hot with shame. I hate my flabby body and limp little breasts with their wide purplish nipples. "Over here," Eli says, guiding me to a mattress on the floor under a sea of India print spreads. The colors all run together, everything blue and grey and Eli climbs on top of me, straddles my hips and rubs my breasts. He gets a little hard and tries to shove it in me, but I'm closed tight. He sucks on his middle finger and puts that in instead, which really hurts, and I flinch though I try not to. "Be cool," he says. He rolls over and gets me on top of him and we do it that way and it works better. He rocks for a while, while I wonder what I'm supposed to be doing with my hips and my hands, my torso swaying above him like a slab of meat. "Sea of Joy" is playing somewhere not too far off, so I concentrate on the words and try to rock in time, but the rhythm keeps changing, the guitars wailing in the back of my skull:

Once the door swings open into space
and I'm already waiting in disguise . . .

By the time the song is over, so are we. Eli rolls me over on my side and he's wiping at the bed with a towel. I stand and put on my dress. It isn't until I walk that I feel the blistering sensation between my legs. Eli shoves his hair out of his face and kisses me once, quick. Then we go back out to the living room where the same freaks are still smoking hash. "Way to go, little brother," says Del. No one looks at me.

I walk home feeling sure that everything must have changed. I search the orderly urban streets, the compact apartment blocks, the shops and the small dirty parks for signs of some new insight, but there is none. All there is is this damp hollow burning between my legs and the buzzing monotone of coming down.

It's maybe 9:30 on a weeknight. We're all home; my parents
are watching TV and I am reading in bed. Dick's been sleeping all day and has refused to come out of his room even for
dinner. All of a sudden, he starts screaming, and before any
of us can get to his room he's gone out the window. Jumped.
My dad dives at the door and wrenches it open; the sash is
pushed wide and the screen torn away. Through the gaping
window, we can see my brother, half-running, half-limping
down the street in his pajamas, lit up and glowing orange
under the streetlamps. Lights switch on in the house next
door. My dad goes charging out our front door to chase
him. My mother hesitates, and then she runs out, too. I slink
back to my room, climb into bed, and put both hands up to
my ears, although it's perfectly silent now in the apartment.
The front door is standing wide open, and the hall light
clicks as it switches itself off. 10 p.m.

My parents fetch my brother from a neighbor's kitchen.
He's banged on their door and ranted to them about a con-
spiracy, told them how my parents have been put up to deal-
ing dope from our apartment—strong-armed into it—and
how the police are in on it, too, but there's been a crackdown
and the police are making a show of it, raiding our apartment with semi-automatic rifles drawn and (breathlessly)
he tells the neighbors how he barely got out in time. They
give him a glass of water and are talking softly to him when
my parents arrive. These are the neighbors who live right
next door to Sylvie and Marie, a drab middle-aged couple
who work at the university and have no kids. Their kindness
astounds me.

*

Dick is a patient on the seventh floor a private psychiatric hospital on Chicago's Near North side. For the first two weeks we aren't allowed to visit him at all. I bake cookies and send them in a tin. The tin comes back the following week with a note, the handwriting shaky, but the sense of humor is distinctly my brother's: "Thanks for the kookies, you kook."

I endure the next five weeks as an only child in a house where the adults who come and go are far too distracted to notice me, but I find opportunity in the vacuum. That's when I first begin to practice the art of leaving by the window.

I wait until my mother switches off the hall light and goes to bed. Then I wait another fifteen or twenty minutes until I can hear my dad's deep breathing, his almost-snores echoing up the hall. In the pitch dark, I part my lace curtains, quietly lift the sash and peel back the screen from its frame. My second-floor room is on the inside of an L-shaped corner of the apartment building. Every third brick juts out from the façade just enough to get a toehold. Below me is a small flat roof above the doorway. I let myself down onto the black tar and scramble the last eight or nine feet down a decorative wrought-iron lattice that frames the entry. My bare feet touch grass and I walk away from the apartment over lawns, avoiding streetlights, feeling the bracing cool of dew-wet grass between my toes. I have pinpricks on my arms and legs, and I tremble with anticipation. At the end of the block, I put on my shoes, which are in the donkey bag slung over my shoulder. The long park that borders Lake Michigan is only five blocks away. In a few minutes, I'll join the other night marauders, the older kids who stay out to smoke pot and watch the shooting stars.

*

One Friday evening after dinner, my mother goes out for a walk and doesn't come back. I'm in my room listening to music on the FM transistor, and I don't pay much attention. I fall asleep with the earphones on, the radio under my pillow. When I wake early the next morning, there's this song from The Band going round and round my head, "take the load off Fanny, take the load for free . . ." My dad is sitting at the table with a cold cup of coffee in front of him. He looks awful, unshaven and unslept. "Do you know where your mother's gone?" he asks me. Is it a question, I wonder, or is he about to tell me? The world slows down, my dad and I alone in a dense fog. "It's summer," he says, talking to himself. "It wouldn't have been very cold last night." We debate calling the police, but in the end we don't. My dad drives around in the car to look for her, and I take the dog and walk down to the lake. Suddenly I need my mother terribly. I am crying as I walk past all the big houses along the lakefront. How could someone simply disappear? For a fleeting moment, I understand that I depend upon my mother the way breathing depends on air.

My mother comes home in the late afternoon. I'm afraid to say anything, but I'm angry too. I stuff it all behind a cool veneer. My dad seems even more anxious than before. "Ivanie," he says, "where have you been?" His voice is husky, like he's choking something back.

"Sitting on a bench. In the park, up near the university."

"What were you doing?" my father asks.

"I was sitting there. Thinking, I guess."

That's all. We eat a meal together in complete silence, just the three of us, that song still stuck in my head. Dick has been away at the hospital for several weeks, but tomorrow they're going to let me see him. If he's having a good day, I can take him out, maybe for a walk around the block. After all, I'm thirteen.

*

A few weeks after my brother went to the hospital, my mother suggested maybe I should see someone too. She'd had a letter from the principal, mailed home with my mid-term report card. It seemed they didn't trust me to deliver it myself. My grades and the teacher's comments indicated several cracks in my reliable, steady demeanor. The letter alerted my parents to my "excessive absences." We had a series of heart-to-heart talks, my mother and I, but for once I wasn't forthcoming. I was curled tight as a pill bug, drawn into myself. "Now you're acting like a teenager," my mother snapped. "Grunts and one-word answers." My cheeks were red hot, but I wasn't giving in.

"I phoned the school," she said. "The guidance counsellor suggested I make an appointment for you at County Mental Health. This Wednesday afternoon at 4, OK? I've arranged with the office to get out early—just this once. You'll have to go on your own after that."

I was secretly pleased. I'd been crawling in my skin, and home was just an empty place I came back to every evening, for the ritual of family dinner and the nightly news. I'd broken up with Eli because I didn't want to have sex again. He was already going out with someone else, not a freak at all, just a nice Jewish girl. She didn't even get high. I suppose I should've been despondent, but I didn't really care. I didn't feel much of anything. I'd taken to stealing again, this time from home: condoms from my dad's sock drawer, money from my mother's purse. I took a twenty-dollar bill and bought an ounce of good pot, rolling joints for all my friends, leaving little treats in their lockers or slipped into their shoes during PE.

On the day of the appointment, my mother read out the

counsellor's name from the information sheet they'd mailed to us: Sister Felipé.

"Holy shit, is she a nun?"

"Language, Abby."

"I'm serious, Mom. I can't talk to a nun."

"She's not just a nun, she's a professional. She talks to kids all the time."

"I'm not a kid."

"Teenager." My mother's voice was strained.

I didn't think how hard it must have been for her to get away from the office more than an hour early, let alone bear the burden of another child on the edge. I wondered if I was cracking up.

My mother announced my arrival to a woman behind a glass screen, and we sat on orange plastic chairs in the waiting room. Across from me, a boy with a round face and broken glasses held together with masking tape had picked up two plastic trucks from the toy corner. He was bashing them together over and over; they were already mangled beyond repair. His mother, a bigger, rounder version of the boy, with stringy hair and bright pink lipstick, swatted the air beside him with a rolled-up magazine. "Cut it out, Henry," she pleaded. "Act your age!"

My name was called, and the woman behind the screen pointed to a room at the end of the corridor. My mother waved to me from her seat and went back to the papers she'd brought from work. The room I entered was small and square. Two chairs set on the diagonal facing each other, a narrow window with half-closed Venetian blinds. Late afternoon sun streamed in unpleasantly. The nun got up from a small desk in the corner, turned and gestured at one of the chairs. She was very little, smaller than me, with a leathery brown face. She wore a white jumper, white stockings, and sported an enormous wooden cross around her neck. Her hair was pulled back in a trim bun. On the wall behind her was that pathetic poster of a kitten dangling from a bar, frantically holding on with its claws. *Hang in there, baby.*

"Sit down, Abby," Sister Felipé said with a quick, tight smile. "Let's get started."

*

I went to Sister Felipé exactly three times. After the third session, the Sister called my mother and told her she thought I was having sex. I didn't know how she'd deduced that, but I was furious. She'd never asked me; I would've told her if she had. Besides, I wasn't having sex. I'd had it once and didn't like it. It wasn't at all like the warm, oceanic encounter I'd dreamed about. It was awkward, boring and messy.

Sister had missed the point entirely. All she'd succeeded in doing was startling my mother and bringing on a few weeks of misplaced scrutiny. I didn't cancel the next appointment. I just never went back.

*

Everything is the wrong way around. When I enter the hospital, the doors are unlocked from the outside. It's easy to breeze right in. But once inside, I quickly discover that the way back out is locked. My mother is waiting in the car; I'm supposed to run back out and tell her when to pick me up. After I check with the nurses on Dick's floor, I have to ask the orderly behind the desk to let me out again. I tell my mother we've got a pass and we're going out for a walk. "Come back in an hour and a half," I say.

"Are you sure you'll be OK, Abby?"

"Yeah, yeah, mom. Fine."

Dick and I take the stairs back down to the lobby. He doesn't want to get in the elevator. The orderly behind the desk looks me up and down. He asks my name and scrutinizes Dick's pass. "Only good for an hour," says the orderly. "You have to have him back here by ten past three." Like he's a sack of laundry or something. I nod my assent and the orderly presses a button underneath the desk. There's a loud click as the lock on the thick glass door releases. Dick shies like a spooked horse.

"It's OK," I say, and give him a big, sure smile. "It's a nice day out there." Dick looks as if he's going to cry, or bolt, so I take him by the hand and lead him towards the door. This time it swings open easily when I lean on the bar.

We step down onto the sidewalk and turn towards the busy intersection. Dick's shaking hard enough to send little tremors up my wrist. "Sorry," he says. "It's the medication." I don't let go of his hand.

There's a crosswalk at the corner, and I plan to take Dick across and into the park. "Come on." I'm making my voice sound as cheerful as possible, but my heart is racing. I look around at the cars that have stopped at the light, and a mixture of pride and embarrassment floods through me. I'm old enough to take my big brother out for a walk, my crazy big brother who hasn't left the hospital for weeks. I wonder what people see when they look at me. Do they know how responsible I am?

Dick's hands are starting to sweat. I suddenly realize that if he panics or tries to run, I won't be able to stop him. We haven't gone ten feet from the hospital door; we aren't even at the corner, when Dick says he wants to go back inside. Something stubborn in me kicks in. "Not yet," I say. "Please—just try to make it to the corner." Dick starts to move again, and a flood of relief surges through me. Maybe I *can* handle this.

At the corner, the lights change against us and we have to wait while cars and taxis whiz past. A black limousine rushes by and Dick goes suddenly rigid. "Now! We have to go back now!"

"But Dick," I tell him. "You can see the lake from the park, just over there." He laughs a nervous little laugh, and says, "Yeah, and the elephants too." But he won't move when the light turns green. I take him back inside.

We sit for a while in the day room, where lots of patients are smoking, but my brother won't let me light up. "What elephants?" I ask, but he doesn't answer. After a while, he says he wants to go to his room, so I lean over and hug him briefly and leave him sitting there. I've failed. I take the elevator back to the lobby, where I thumb through wilted issues of *Time Magazine*, waiting for my mother to pick me up.

*

My brother was home by Thanksgiving, but he wasn't back in school. He'd crushed a vertebra when he jumped and had to wear a stiff brace on his back. It was itchy and uncomfortable, but he couldn't stand without it. He had some kind of home study course he would work on in the evenings with my parents' help, and two young men came by a few afternoons a week. One was a divinity school student, the other studied business administration at Northwestern. They were supposed to be helping my brother cope, but between the back brace and all the medication, Dick mostly slept. I took it on as my project to cheer him up.

On the days when I wasn't over at the Andersen's, or off

at the park scoring dope and getting high, I would come home and knock on Dick's door. If he was awake, I'd go in and perch on the end of his bed and read his poems and listen to music. I went Christmas shopping for him, getting gag gifts for mom and dad, a rawhide chew toy shaped like a small Christmas stocking for the dog, and a red catnip mouse for the cat. I offered to get my brother stoned, but he just shook his head and said, "No way."

I persuaded my father to let us make the annual photo album by ourselves. In the past, my father always posed us in front of the fireplace or by the Christmas tree. We'd add the new photo and wrap it up and gave it to my mother under the tree. Every year, she'd act surprised. Then we'd all sit next to her, as she looked through the album, page by page, until she came to the new photo and exclaimed in delight. The album was a tidy record of holiday outfits and the passing of our childhoods.

Our first decision was that we should each get a page of our own, to do with as we pleased. When we were done, the staid old Christmas album exploded with psychedelic intensity, our pages thickly decorated with cut-up photos, layers of pictures and headlines from *Rolling Stone* and *Mad Magazine*. Dick's featured a pen-and-ink portrait of Bob Dylan and the words "roughing it." Mine had a photo of me in an old Army jacket, taken from behind. I'm swivelled around to face the camera, my lips in a puffy grimace, my pupils dilated. The photo was adorned at the top by a tiny clipping from the New Yorker that said, "Last chance to set a young person straight."

*

It's a novel way to drop out.

In the fall of 1972, after just a few weeks at high school, I start ditching a new class every week. First, I cut PE, then skip out on math, biology, history, French. Keep up the drama elective until they want me to try out for a play. Don't show up for the audition; get high in the park with Tony and Mark instead. Keep up with English and art until I'm too high to read my watch. Ditch most of those classes too. I'm too far behind to catch up now; soon there's no point in going to class at all. It's such a big school nobody seems to notice. The teachers, I imagine, figure I've transferred out or moved away. The people in the office are too busy to care.

Think I'm the only person in the history of Evanston Township High School who is too mild-mannered to expel. At the end of the year, when they finally catch on to me and my parents are called in for a conference, they simply hand my mother a list of alternative schools. Private schools. Expensive. "Perhaps this isn't the best environment for your daughter," is all they say.

*

Robin is practicing Tai Chi in the park the first time I see him. He moves like a lizard under a hot lamp, achingly slow, his arms cutting wide circles in the bright sun. I'm stoned, as usual, and have no idea what he's doing, so I stare. When he finishes his last move—a great sweeping arc of the body, muscles taut, pulling trails of air like heavy cloth through water—Robin turns to me and lifts his eyes. He's the most beautiful person I've ever seen: all over, the color of sand.

Even though he's looking right at me he doesn't seem to see me. I have to turn away to suppress a goofy wave.

On Saturday, I have a date with Linda and Ann. Ann's got some tabs of blotter acid, little hearts on a piece of vellum paper, and we're dropping them and going to the movies. We're going to see Frank Langella in *The Twelve Chairs* for the third or fourth time. I've had a crush on Frank Langella since the movie first came out, a crush eclipsed only by my infatuation with George, the quiet Beatle.

On the way out of the theatre, Ann says "Let's go down to the Lake." We're tripping our asses off at this point, too far gone to take the bus. Linda's lost her legs back in the dark theatre; she says no problem, she'll float all the way. We walk east past the library towards the Northwestern campus. I think I see Robin on the library steps, and I make us all double back to see if he's really there. But the library is closed, and no one's around. On campus, the dark brick buildings are expanding and contracting, creaking like old men settling in chairs. "Breathing like houses," Ann says and we all nod. We know exactly what she means. We duck into Amazing Grace, and I think I see Robin at a table near the front. The room's crowded, even though no one's on stage, and we squeeze through the tables and chairs at my insistence. Linda trips and falls to her knees and we have to help her up. She's laughing so hard tears are streaming down her face. When we finally get to the front, the table's empty, just a dirty coffee mug and a half-eaten sandwich left on a plate. "He's haunting you," Ann says.

The acid lasts and lasts, and we keep walking. It's too dangerous for Linda to go home to her suspicious, uptight parents. We walk Ann down to her apartment near the Howard Street L, and Linda and I make our way back up to my place as the sun sets and porch lights come on. We stop at a phone booth and Linda calls home, begs permission to spend the night with me. I can hear her pleading and bargaining inside the box. My legs are tired, and I've got a dull ache in my stomach. I'm probably hungry, but eating is still out of the question. At home, we tell my mother we've had dinner at Ann's, and we go straight to my room. We light a candle and sit facing each other on opposite ends of the bed, my Scottish wool blanket stretched between us, a universe of lavender stars. We tell each other stories about where we came from and where we're going. I'm reciting "Winken, Blinken, and Nod" when my mother opens the door and peers in. "Are you girls all right?"

"Yeah, mom. Just talking."

"Let me see your faces," my mother says. She snaps on the light, strides over to the bed and takes my chin in her hand.

"You girls were smoking something."

"No, mom," I protest. And then, in a stroke of rare genius, I say, "We met up with Mark and his friends down at the Lake. *They* were smoking something. They said it was marijuana, but I think it was catnip or something. We tried it, but nothing happened. Really."

My mother looks at me with narrowed eyes. Her skin glows a soft orange, patterned like leaves, with tiny interconnected pathways running into her hair and down her neck. The halo of light around her head is pulsating. "That's not very smart, is it? We'll talk about it in the morning." She blows out the candle on the bedside table, turns off the light and shuts the door behind her. "Now go to sleep."

*

I conspired to meet Robin in the usual places, but it wasn't easy. I dug around, asked questions of the freaks I hung out with in the park. There wasn't much to go on. Robin was seventeen; he'd dropped out of school to study with a Chinese master. "Study what?" I asked his little brother Mark who sold me white crosses and black beauties for fifty cents a pop. "How to walk softly and carry a big stick," Mark said, grinning. He told me how Robin practiced Tai Chi all the time and meditated, too. I kept coming back to the place I'd first seen him, but he wasn't often there. He was all mystery: no regular habits, no favorite haunts.

Occasionally Robin joined our circle and smoked pot with us. Sometimes we'd go for a walk, but Robin never said much, and I'd squirm in the long silences. Or I'd get nervous and brag about all the drugs I'd done. Even as I said it, I knew I sounded silly and immature. I tried to quiet down and pay attention, but Robin was a puzzle I couldn't quite work out. When he walked in his soft suede moccasins, his footsteps made no sound at all.

I borrowed Marie's yoga book and went into my closet with a candle and tried to meditate. My mind wasn't quiet enough for that. Either I was on my way up or on my way down and in between I was hyper, lusty, angry, sad—full of wanting and contradictions.

One night towards the end of summer, I slipped out the window and found myself alone under the trees at South Street beach. I leaned back on my hands and watched dense patches of cloud shift across a marquee of motionless stars. Lit up a joint and smoked deeply, trapping the scaly heat in my throat and lungs for as long as I could stand it. The night breeze lifted at my clothes, prickled my skin. I felt a presence and turned to see Robin standing just a few feet away. I sat up with a start. He moved towards me slowly, as if he was still doing Tai Chi. Asked me what I was doing there. I offered him the joint, which had gone out, but he shook his head. He sat down next to me, and I pointed up at the moving layer of clouds and the fixed layer of stars beyond and tried to explain what I'd seen when I was tripping. How space stripped away in thin transparent planes, splitting off around me in all directions, like screens on which the world was projected—sidewalks, houses, cars, trees: all movies, lucent and transitory. How I tried to slip between them and never could. Robin said nothing. "What about you?" I asked. Robin pointed to the sky where the clouds had parted, and the stars were starting to move. "Perseids," he said.

The sky was suddenly alive with dropping and fizzing stars and we leaned back and watched the meteor shower for a long time without speaking. It must've been two, maybe three in the morning when Robin took me by the hand and led me down onto the sand, out of sight of the headlights of police cruisers that occasionally drove the park paths looking for kids like us. He wrapped his arms around me and kissed me once, very softly, on the lips. He spread his flannel shirt on the sand, and we lay on it, side by side. I was stiff with fear, sure he'd reject me. My flabby stomach, my dense thoughts. Fucked-up as usual. I could hear each breath as if I were gulping air. But he kissed me again and we kissed and kissed and kissed.

I woke, chilly and damp, in a hollow of sand. Robin, a few paces away, was doing Tai Chi in the first light of dawn. I put my fingers to my mouth, sure I'd been dreaming, but my lips were sore and slightly puffy. It hurt when I smiled.

The next day Robin came to my house. I was reading in bed when I saw him standing motionless under my window. He'd brought me a copy of a book by Shunryu Suzuki: *Zen Mind, Beginner's Mind*. Immediately I abandoned the Tolkein I'd been trying to slog through because everyone else was reading it, and I switched to Zen.

Suzuki seemed to be telling me I didn't exist. My "original mind" was empty and an empty mind was a ready mind.

This had something—or everything—to do with freedom. It sounded good, but I was too full of desires. My version of freedom would be much more cluttered. I wanted Robin to love me, or at the very least have sex with me. I wanted him to *want* me. Except for Eli, no one had ever shown an interest. Until now. Maybe. But with Robin it was hard to tell. He turned up or he didn't. He might hold my hand and he might not. Sometimes we kissed. He told me he was trying to preserve his chi, which was some kind of life force, like an electric current in his bloodstream. When he didn't turn up, there was nothing at all. It was no use going by his house. I did it once. His mother just sighed and offered me a drink of water. She was kneading bread on a giant wooden board. "I have no idea where my boys have gone," she said, punching the dough half-heartedly.

I settled for getting high and out of my skin—so often that I lost count. Even Tony, who sold the best hallucinogens in the park, tried to slow me down. "You're just a kid," he said, refusing to sell me some tabs of Orange Sunshine. He put a fatherly hand on my shoulder. "You need to take it easy. Take some time off." I was proud as hell of earning Tony's concern. I gave him a big hug and walked away, belting it out just like Janis: "Freedom's just another word for nothin' left to lose."

"She's gone, man," Tony yelled after me. "Long gone."

Departures

1973-1976

Thursday June 6.

Dear Mom, Dad & Abby...

It just flashed in my mind when I was writing the date - how interesting and strange it is to know what I I was thinking about - what we all were thinking about - exactly 6 years ago. It seems like such a short period in the world's history. But it's such a large ~~shoot~~ chunk out of our lives - 6 years!

Scott and I are fine. Living here is fun and interesting but I find that I don't get the privacy I enjoy as people - my friends, Scott's friends, and Abby's friends - are always traipsing in and out. By the way - I have turned out to be the compulsively neat one of the two of us - Scott doesn't care about all kinds of (minor but important) chores like washing dishes and washing floors and cleaning up - but I do.

We moved to Lexington, Massachusetts, on August 31, 1973. Lexington was a classic suburban backwater, a thousand miles from Evanston and light years apart. None of the kids lounging around the donut shop or driving too fast up and down Mass Ave seemed to be interested in anything other than cars or football. Girls my age had big hair and wore make-up. Even the stoners looked like they preferred Quaaludes or were just naturally stupid. There were no freaks like me. It looked like the Summer of Love never happened in Lexington.

My parents chose the town for the school. It was supposed to be one of the best in the area, and not nearly as big as ETHS. Maybe I wouldn't get lost in it—at least that was the idea. My dad had graduated from Lexington High. He was a track star, and he went on to an Ivy League college. All this seemed to matter; it was discussed in my entrance interview, along with my "spotty" academic history. I was ready to make a case for myself, to tell them I wanted a fresh start. But the principal just stood and shook my dad's hand and sent me off down the hall to the guidance counsellor to sort out my schedule. Miss Gregg recommended a few extra classes each term. "That ought to do it," she said, handing me my timetable with an efficient smile. "We'll have you graduating with your class."

Dick had gone off to college in the White Mountains of New Hampshire. Franconia was a tiny school, not even accredited. It was only a few hours away, but it seemed like a distant oasis. He was studying beat poetry and philosophy and he'd already landed a late-night slot on the college radio station.

And I was alone.

*

On Friday, September 13, Gramma Down died. My mother flew out to Sioux City immediately, and my dad and I followed the next day. Gramma Down had been bad for years. In the end, the disease left her without speech, with very little movement. She lay all day in a reclined chair in the harsh artificial light of the nursing home corridor, where the attendants could keep an eye on her. Her mouth hung open, drool pooling on the folds of her dressing gown. Her skin the color of uncooked potatoes.

My grandfather was a prominent surgeon, head of the hospital. He was respected in the community. Well-liked. "What a terrible shame about Alice," people said, admiring my grandfather living as a bachelor all those years, visiting Alice every day. Maintaining his sense of humor.

*

My mother is ironing a large white tablecloth in preparation for the onslaught of well-wishers. Aunt Karen sits with her fists balled up on the table in front of her. She and my mother are talking in low voices about the autopsy. "I can't understand it: he's a doctor, for God's sake, a man of science." Grampa Down has refused the autopsy. "Without it, we'll never know exactly what killed her." Pictures of my Gramma when she was young, beautifully dressed in immaculately tailored clothes, are spread all over the table. My aunt is fingering them and crying. My mother's jaw is set like stone.

My dad says it's the first and only time he's ever seen them angry with their father. Gramma Down will be buried tomorrow, vacant and lifeless, with her body still intact.

*

Even after we moved to Lexington and I had no friends to hang out with, nowhere to go, and no drugs to buy, I continued stealing from my mother's purse. Usually I just took change, sometimes dollars, occasionally a five. My mother always left her purse on the kitchen counter near the phone, and I rifled through it when she was in the bathroom or reading *The New Yorker* on the couch. I didn't need the money; it was just habit, a small diversion. I'd never been caught.

After the funeral, my mother started a new job at Crittenton-Hastings, a home for unwed mothers that also operated a controversial abortion clinic. She was responsible for fundraising. The head physician at the clinic, Dr. Edelin had been convicted of manslaughter in 1971. He'd performed a legal abortion, but one of the technicians in the room claimed to have seen the foetus breathing and raised the alarm. A higher court promptly overturned the manslaughter charge, and Dr. Edelin was exonerated, but even the most liberal donors, my mother said, were afraid to be associated with the place. She brought home piles of work every night.

My mother started to drink. Most nights after dinner, she sat at the dining room table working on budgets and appeal letters. I sat with her and wrestled with my homework. She drank while she worked until she nodded off, slumped over in her chair. Sometimes I had to nudge her and tell her to go to bed. Sometimes, when my dad wasn't around, if she was drinking wine, she'd offer me a glass. Sometimes she'd get sloppy and talk too much, slurring her words and making little sense.

One night, she started talking about my dad. There was some complicated stuff about money—she seemed to be accusing him of compulsive spending, of pledging money we didn't have to places like his alumni association so he could look good in front of his old school friends. She said it was all appearances. I didn't get it. My dad wasn't that kind of person. Then she told me how unsatisfactory their sex life had been. I was so embarrassed; I tried not to listen. I sat stony-faced and gulped down the wine she'd poured in my glass. She was just telling me how she and my dad made sure to have sex at least once a week, on Saturday nights, when I heard my dad's car in the driveway. I stood up, a little wobbly, and rushed into the kitchen with our glasses and the empty bottle, then disappeared upstairs to my little attic room. In the morning, my mother was drinking black coffee and scowling in the kitchen. She had a headache, but she seemed to have forgotten our conversation. At least, she never mentioned it again.

*

I was sitting outside school during study period with my biology text cracked open in my lap, when I saw my father drive into the parking lot. He cruised up next to me and rolled the window down, ignored the cigarette I was quickly stubbing out, and asked me if I wanted to come for a drive. He walked me to the office and made some sort of excuse, smiling and shaking hands with the school secretary.

I grabbed my things from my locker, and we were off. It was an hour up to Rockport. His office was near a pier lined with souvenir shops and galleries. My dad gave me a bit of money and told me to wander around and have some fun. I bought a cheesy little driftwood sculpture and a purple plastic lighter that said "Historic Rockport" with a picture of a seagull perched on a piling. I sat and smoked at the end of the pier, flicking the lighter off and on.

After my dad finished at the office, he came to find me on the pier. We bought some fried clams in a take-out container and walked down on the rocky beach. The sun had already set behind the hills when we headed back to the car. "Don't tell your mother," my dad said as he pulled out onto the highway. I smiled at my reflection in the window and the black trees rushing by.

*

It's like we were trying to feel like a family, going through the motions. I got the bright idea that maybe I should start cooking dinner for everyone. I spent hours in the kitchen after school, trying out the recipes in *Diet for a Small Planet*, the stereo blasting from the other room. When my mother came home, she'd go immediately in and turn the music down. She said Neil Young couldn't sing to save his life, but she admitted to liking some of his songs. Once I walked into the living room with the dust rag, and caught my mother leaning on the vacuum handle, swaying and singing along to "Walk on the Wild Side."

*

One Sunday morning we went apple picking. We filled a big bushel basket and a couple of paper shopping bags and spent the rest of the day cutting and peeling and sweating over the canning racks. My mother lowered a packed jar into the boiling water too quickly and it split open with a loud crack. Globs of applesauce clouded the sterile bath. My mother swore and started to cry and my dad strode in from the other room and said, "Jesus Christ, Ivanie, what's the big deal?" I retreated upstairs and wrote a long letter to my brother, telling him I thought I was going crazy all by myself with "the parents."

Dick wrote back immediately:

Abby: please come as soon as possible!!! Bring apples!

Love, Dick

So off I went on the bus up to Franconia for a weekend visit. Dick's roommate, Chad, didn't seem to mind if I crashed on a borrowed mattress on the floor between their beds. Chad had a great stereo, and between them they had a record collection that filled an entire wall. The school was housed in an old Victorian hotel on a hillside: classrooms, dorm rooms, dining hall, everything in one building. Kids lounged around on sprung easy chairs in the dilapidated splendour of the common room, with its mangy velvet drapes and threadbare carpets. They argued politics and plotted an organic garden to feed the school. My brother had a girl-friend, but she had other boyfriends too. Everybody lived together and no one seemed to mind. I should've felt happy there but instead I felt lonelier than ever.

I told Dick about Mom and the drinking, about what she said about Dad and the money, but I didn't mention the sex stuff. He just shook his head and said, "Yeah, she's done that to me too. The last time I was home, after you went to bed, I stayed up talking with her." My brother couldn't drink because of the medication he was on, so he was perfectly sober when my mother ambushed him. "She told me she's absolutely sure she's going to die of the same illness that her mother died of, and her mother's mother. You know, her cousin Shirley Ruth's got it now too." My brother's voice went quiet. "I think she's really scared. You know, I am too."

I'd never thought of it that way before. The *family* illness. It could get my mother. It could get my brother and me too. Dick said, "I'm never having children. I'm not passing *that* any further."

On Saturday night, I sat quietly in the makeshift sound booth in a broom closet in the basement of Franconia. Dick's show had been shifted to the prime slot, nine to midnight. He leaned into the microphone: "This is Dick Joslin, coming to you live from the White Mountains of New Hampshire on radical radio, W-O-M-B." Toward the end of the show, Dick let me spin a couple of disks. I played "Sisters of Mercy" and Neil Young's "Everybody Knows this is Nowhere," dedicated to my nowhere life.

The weekend ended too soon. When I got home, I felt worse than ever. It was awful having no one to talk to. My mother continued drinking, and I tried not to hang around the dining room table after dinner anymore. All the cooking and baking I did to fill in the hours after school before my parents came home was doing me no favors. I was getting fat. I couldn't fit into half of my clothes.

One afternoon, after school, I took the bus into Arlington Center and caught the Red Line to Harvard Square. I'd always relied on Sylvie and Marie and their sixth sense for second-hand chic in matters of fashion. Now I was going it alone. I found a brown leather cap in a grungy second-hand shop, a matching vest and boots that laced up to my knees. I bought a pair of tight, straight-legged jeans and some big silver hoop earrings. It all looked great in the store, but when I got home and showed my mother, she said the leather was fake. It was a bit too thin and shiny. I hadn't even noticed. I laced the boots up over the tight jeans and looked in the mirror. I looked like a stuffed sausage, or worse, like a bit player in *Shaft*, a wanna-be something I wasn't. I shoved the boots, the hat, and the vest under my bed, and tucked the earrings in my sock drawer.

Sylvie sent a letter with a picture of herself and her new boyfriend on a camping trip. They were both wearing oversized flannel shirts and hiking boots and Sylvie looked beautiful, like a wood nymph, her miraculous hair floating around her in a halo of strawberry light. I dug around in the attic for my father's old L.L. Bean shirts, and that became my uniform. A big flannel shirt was a good place to hide.

*

In the spring of 1974, I went back up to Franconia again. Dick told me he was planning to spend the summer in Evanston. His old friend Scott had a studio apartment in Rogers Park and Dick was going to live there. He was going to get a job and try to save some money, and he'd already made plans to ship a bunch of his records. He was buying Chad's stereo off of him at the end of term. He said, "Hey, why don't you come out for the summer?"

That weekend, we cooked up a plan. Dick wrote to Scott, and I wrote to Sylvie and Marie to tell them the good news.

Franconia got out nearly a month before Lexington High, so Dick was going to be the vanguard: he'd get there first and get it all set up for me. I'd pulled As and Bs in a couple of subjects, and I hadn't failed anything, not even algebra. I thought there was a good chance I could convince my parents that I was responsible enough to go.

*

Dick arrived in Chicago on May 17 to a near-disaster when the greyhound bus disgorged the stereo with its tone arm broken and one of the speakers gone mute. Luckily Scott had a soldering gun and a little know-how, and the music was back on in the space of a day. Dick's first letter was long and rambling. He mentioned all my friends: Sylvie, Marie, their parents, Linda, Ann, Holden. Dick told us he'd landed a job at Jay's Diner as a cook: he wasn't being paid yet, just trained, and although he admitted making lots of mistakes, and he said he was angry at Jay for being so tough and condescending, he sounded upbeat about the prospects. He described the apartment, and the people he'd seen:

> Abby, everyone asks for you and wishes you well. I accidentally bumped into Mark S. a couple of nights ago and I don't see why you like(d) him. He seems like a real phony and crazy-stupid person. He had just an hour before been jumped at Foster Beach by two guys. He was attempting to sell them Quaaludes, the idiot, and they broke his nose and stole them (the Quaaludes). I felt sorry for him, though . . . . As a matter of fact, I have met very few sane people here, very, very few. We met our neighbors the other night, they came over and we had a party. I had about ten tequila sunrises. It was darling. Our neighbors turn out to be: Al, across the hall, who's gay and was in the peace corps in India, Rob who lives across the court and is also gay, Tad and David downstairs (Tad sells drugs and told me he can get me anything I want) . . .

A week or so before I was supposed to climb on the greyhound bus, my parents were still wavering. I'd already shipped my records and a few books (*Zen Mind, Beginner's Mind, Be Here Now* and the handmade compilation of poetry and quotations that Sylvie had given me when I moved away). My duffle bag was packed. I had the bus fare; I'd saved that by not spending my allowance and by other less honest means. My mother wanted to know if I had a plan. I told her I'd talked with our old neighbors, the Coles about house-sitting for the month of August, which left me with only six or seven weeks to fill in with some acceptable activity, like a job. "Linda thinks she can get me a waitressing job," I said, wondering if maybe she could.

Another letter arrived and I ripped it open and read it before my parents came home. Dick described the apartment and the neighborhood just South of Evanston, an area a bit rougher than where I was accustomed to living. It sounded exciting to me, but I couldn't imagine what my parents would think. I left the letter on the kitchen counter and hoped for the best.

> I've done some thinking and have decided that it's OK for Abby to come and live as long as she realizes that we're a block or two from a half-way dangerous area. (There's always room for one more in this apt.) I realize that Abby will be wanting to stay at friends' houses 'til late and I don't want her to feel that I'm a parent to her. I feel she is mature enough to take responsibility for her own safety. So, she is welcome here as long as she understands there are risks involved and that she herself is responsible for making judgements for herself on what is safe and wise to do at any time.

Astonishingly, my parents agreed. As soon as I finished my end of year exams, I was on my way. It was a long two days on a Greyhound bus, and I couldn't read for more than a few minutes without getting queasy. Stopping all night at little towns on the outskirts of nowhere, I piled out with my fellow passengers and stretched, poked around to see if the restrooms behind the gas station were any cleaner than the claustrophobic WC on the bus. From Rochester to Cleveland, two men in the seat across from me passed a bottle in a brown paper bag between them. One of them coughed a rattling, phlegmy cough, and they both got off and smoked silently at every stop. Somewhere southwest of Indianapolis, in the grey light of dawn the bus made an unscheduled stop on the side of a two-lane highway. The men retrieved old felt hats from the rack above, climbed down off the bus—no luggage or anything—and wandered off down the road. The driver told us we could all get out and stretch, and I did. There was a boarded-up service station, and across the road a house with the porch light on. A bird called from somewhere behind the service station and was answered by its mate in a tall tree across the road. A light snapped on inside the little house. I looked back down the road, bordered on both sides by cornfields. The men had vanished without a trace.

I slept a bit from Indianapolis to the Illinois border, but shook myself awake for the descent into Chicago along the Skyway, past the dirty backs of tenement houses strung with laundry, past factories with cracked and broken windows. The cityscape rolled on below us for what seemed like ages until we came to the crest of the Skyway and the skyscrapers of Chicago bloomed out the left-hand windows of the bus. In the distance, Lake Michigan was a long blue smudge on the horizon. Just shy of downtown, the bus rolled off the Skyway, ground down through its gears, brakes exhaling into the Greyhound station. Dick was standing at the head of the empty slot where our bus was headed, wearing flip-flops and denim shorts and a shirt with big blue and white flowers splashed all over it. He shielded his eyes with his right hand, shoulders hunched, and squinted into the sun.

I spent the first night on a thin mattress on the floor. Things scuttled around me in the dark, troubling my sleep. In the morning, I faced a stuck-on mass of dishes in the sink and decided the place just had to be cleaned. Linda came by before breakfast, took one look around the tiny apartment with a shocked expression, and the two of us headed out to the grocery store to buy bleach and cleanser and heavy-duty sponges.

I wanted to get some bread dough going first—I'd been bragging about my new culinary skills—so Linda started sweeping and mopping the studio while I punched and kneaded some dough into shape at the tiny linoleum table in the kitchen. I turned on the oven to make a nice warm place for the dough to rise, and hundreds of cockroaches poured out of the back, streamed up the walls and fanned out across the floor. I ran screaming from the room, grabbed Linda and my purse and slammed the front door with my heart thumping. "Gross!" we both squealed, and the guy across the hall opened his door and asked what the fuss was all about.

"Raid," he said dispassionately, when I breathlessly explained what'd happened. Like it was no big deal. Like it happened all the time.

*

I didn't last long at Dick and Scott's apartment. First it was my friends that irritated Dick: he said he thought they were

96

mostly all losers, selfish and fucked up. Then the crowded conditions started to bother him. After only a week or two, Dick asked me to find somewhere else to stay. I didn't mind. I could always crash at Sylvie's and Marie's in a pinch.

That afternoon, I ran into Maggie at Lake Street beach. Maggie was a couple of years older than me, a folk singer. She grew up in Evanston, but she'd been on the road for a while, driving around in an Econoline van, playing her guitar and singing for tips in bars and cafés. She was sitting under a tree with her guitar in her lap, telling stories about the road. There was a rumor going around that Maggie was bisexual, that she'd even had a fling with Linda and with Holden too—my latest crush. I was too embarrassed to ask Linda, but the mystique surrounding Maggie had me mesmerized. I hung on her every word.

Maggie asked me where I was living, and when I told her nowhere, she said I could come live at The House if I wanted. The House was a notorious hippie pad on Simpson, near downtown Evanston. That summer, Mushroom and Goldberry were living there while they fixed up their magic bus. Wild man Dirk was there too, and a handful of other freaks came and went between music festivals and Dead concerts.

I moved in later the same day. Maggie drove me up, with my records and my duffle bag in the back of her van. She had a picture of a Hindu god on the dashboard, and a mattress in the back. "For the road," she said.

Goldberry was presiding in the kitchen when we arrived. Somebody had lifted a crate of peaches off a loading dock and they were being made into pies and preserves. A short, round girl named Lucy, dressed from head to toe in what looked like tie-dyed scarves, worked at the stove. A couple of lanky guys sorted peaches, tossing the rotten ones in a bin. Mushroom was sitting cross-legged in the corner with a book in his lap, stroking his beard and ignoring everyone. "Go on upstairs," Goldberry said, smiling and touching my arm with her slender fingers. "Dirk and Tammy and Ben are hopping in the shower. You hop in too, get clean, then come join us in Mother Nature's kitchen." There was a little burst of appreciative laughter and Goldberry beamed around the room.

Outside on the back lawn, a scrawny guy with long matted hair was jumping up and down and yelping. I couldn't tell if he was happy or hurt. "What's with him?" I asked, but Goldberry just nodded her head towards the stairs and went back to her peaches.

I got used to communal showers with loofahs and Dr. Bronner's Peppermint Soap. Nothing in The House was ever done alone. I slept on a big futon on the floor of an otherwise empty bedroom. There were usually two or three people sharing the bed with me. Sometimes Marie crashed at The House. She was mad at her parents all the time and thinking of dropping out and hitching out west. Mushroom said she could come on the bus "when the winds changed," his euphemism for when he finished re-building the engine. The House was notorious for once allowing only Grateful Dead records on the stereo, but Marie and Maggie were changing that, jamming to folk music and listening to scratchy blues and bluegrass records.

Dirk was my favorite in The House. He was the only person with a real job; he worked as a handyman in a big block of apartments in Rogers Park. He had a huge bunch of keys on a chain clipped to his belt and was hyper and funny and wickedly smart. He treated me like a puppy, looking out for me and making sure no one took advantage of me. No one did, of course. That's not what it was like at The House.

I knew I should look for work, but it was too much fun

just bumming around, waiting for Dirk to show up, going for rides in his truck to places I'd never been before: north to Winnetka and Glencoe, where we drove through deep forested ravines at breakneck speed with all the windows rolled down, or into town to play the "Occupations" game. We'd pull up to an intersection and spot a pedestrian about to cross. Dirk would say, "What does he do?" and I would have to guess.

"Accountant, maybe?"

"No," said Dirk. "Piano tuner." Then he'd lean out the window with his disarming grin and say, "Excuse me—can I ask what you do for a living?"

"I'm a pianist," said the man. "And I tune pianos."

Dirk was nearly always right.

*

A week after I moved to The House, Dick told me he was planning to move, too. Scott was a slob and, for the first time in his life, my brother found he was the neat one. Scott couldn't hold a job either. He kept borrowing money for food. Dick said Scott was acting paranoid. "He keeps telling me how his mother tried to poison him. He says that's why he's so fucked up," my brother told me over coffee one morning. I couldn't help wondering about Dick and Scott, who used to be best friends. Which one of them was really paranoid? A guy Dick knew, a jazz pianist, was going on the road and offered to sublet his apartment to Dick. It was a tiny place, overlooking the tracks near the Chicago Street L in Evanston. Dick had landed a job at a medical records company in the Loop, so he wasn't flipping burgers and being yelled at by Jay anymore. He seemed happy enough, but I thought he might be getting a little hyper. He was allowed to wear sandals to work, and he painted his toenails bright blue to get a rise out of his supervisor. He was juggling two girlfriends, and they were sisters. I didn't know if it was such a good idea for Dick to live alone, but I didn't spend too much time thinking about it. If I had, I might've been envious of his happiness. But I didn't think it was my place to judge.

Sylvie had a summer job painting houses with her boyfriend. She was working all the time, and at night she was too tired to stay out late. Marie went to a women's music festival with Maggie and they stayed out on the road for a couple of weeks. Sylvie's parents were more lenient than ever. They let her stay over at Danny's house—she'd practically moved in, and the two of them were bickering like an old married couple.

There was sex going on all around me, but as usual I wasn't having any. I hung around Holden's place far more than I should, trying to attract his attention. I left anonymous notes with sultry Billie Holiday lyrics under his pillow ("I am only what you make me, come take me, I'm yours."). Holden didn't seem to mind having me there, he just didn't seem to notice me much. I felt like wallpaper or a comfortable chair. He was mad about bicycle racing, trying to get into condition for some big event. Gangly, intense cycling guys were always hanging around his basement bedroom, giving him a hand with his spokes and gears. I tried but was never able to get Holden alone.

*

On Sundays, I went to a pay phone near the library and called home. My parents would get on the phone at the same time and pepper me with questions. "Have you found a job?" (Still looking.) "How are Sylvie and Marie?" (Good.) "Tell us about the place you're staying." (It's nice. The people there are really cool.) "Are you getting enough to eat?" (Yeah. We have communal dinners at The House.) I waved the word *communal* like a little flag: see how grown-up I am? "How's Dick?" (Fine, he's fine.) "Well, then. Are you looking for a job?"

I always said goodbye in a hurry but walked away from the phone booth feeling restless and sad.

One Sunday, I didn't go back to The House after the weekly call. I walked down to the lake instead and south along the beaches and parks. Turned west and wandered the streets of my old neighborhood until I found myself on the Andersens' steps. Lorraine was in the kitchen, trying to carve a chicken. She swore at the carving knife and threw it in the sink before she spotted me hovering in the doorway. She shrugged her shoulders impishly, ducked her head, and gave me a conspiratorial grin. "Oh, Ah-bee!" she said with great excitement and threw her arms around me like I was her long-lost daughter. I burst into tears.

*

It's what that summer was like. Unsettled, constantly adrift. I didn't know how to be alone and on my own. Everything I tried felt empty. My friends were all older than me. Sure of themselves. Everyone had a plan, or, like Goldberry, they didn't need one. I worked for a while in a fancy old folks' home, waiting tables in the formal dining room. Some of the residents were mean. Others were just sad and pathetic. I hated the way it smelled, of urine and bleach and something else—the smell of people who are unloved, unlovable. I think I lasted three weeks before quitting.

In August, I moved into the Coles' apartment to look after their four cats while they travelled in Mexico. I was extremely relieved to get out of The House. Dirk had moved on, Maggie was still on the road, and I just couldn't take Mother Nature any longer. Nothing was ever a problem in Goldberry's world; she rejected even the slightest complaint. Some of my things, records and clothes, had gone missing. I suspected Maggie's girlfriend, who took off one day without a word, but there was no way to pursue it in that fairy tale atmosphere.

I settled in and started eating my way through the Coles' pantry, well stocked with delicious lemon biscuits, gourmet soups and homemade jams. The Coles left money for cat food, and some extra for me. I walked up to the supermarket on Chicago Ave and stocked the fridge. Friends came over. We spent long afternoons in the sun, stroking the cats and listening to Shawn Phillips, trying to unravel the hypnotic complexity of the lyrics.

At night, we smoked pot, made big meals, and drank wine until well after midnight. One night, Holden was still there after everyone else left. I thought maybe I'd kiss him, maybe ask him to stay, but it turned out he just wanted to talk to me about Sylvie. She was breaking up with Danny, and Holden wanted to know if she might go out with him. I said something vague and encouraging. Holden gave me a quick relieved hug and backed out the door. I cried myself to sleep.

*

Dick turns up at the Coles' apartment on a Saturday afternoon in mid-August. He looks terrible, like he hasn't slept in days. I stand back to let him in and he peers around nervously. "Is anyone here?" he asks. I assure him I'm alone and lead him, shaking, into the living room. Immediately he asks me to pull the blinds. I have a bad feeling about this. He sits on the couch hugging his legs with his arms and asks me for a Bible. I can't think what he'd want a Bible for, but I go searching for one anyway. Dick follows me, ranting about judgement and the apocalypse as I paw frantically through all the bookcases. I search the closets and the drawers of the bedside tables. I even look in Susan Cole's underwear drawer. No Bible.

Dick is seriously agitated. It's like little bits of him are flying away at odd angles. He won't sit down; he's moving all around the apartment and scaring the cats. Dick suspects them of some kind of unspecified malevolence. They're skittering away from Dick, pinging off corners and skidding on the hall rugs as he paces the floor. The little one, Inocencia, is already hiding under the spare bed. Dick's sure something terrible is happening, and not just to him. There's no talking him down. "I need the Bible," he wails, and clutches his head, cowering in a corner of the spare room. In desperation, I get my copy of *Be Here Now*, which I've gotten sick of reading because it reminds me too much of Goldberry, Miss Love and Light. I sit down on the spare bed and coax Dick to sit next to me. I hold open the book so he can see the first page with its cheerful hand-lettered quips of easy wisdom. I read for a few minutes before Dick's up and out the door again, pacing, moaning, questioning, accusing.

Things happen too fast. Marie comes to the apartment, and I stop her at the door, saying, "Don't come in, it's Dick, he's really bad. Can you call Scott?" She fetches Scott and Sylvie too, but the four of us together can't calm him down. Marie tries boiling up a pot of spaghetti, but Dick won't eat it. Marie gets pissed off and goes off into the night, leaving a sink full of dishes. I'm trying to clean up when Scott comes into the kitchen and says, "We tripped yesterday, split a 4-way hit of windowpane. Dick had a really bad time. Death and rebirth, you know. He was talking to spirits. I think it's happening all over again."

I'm afraid something really bad is going to happen. Dick's going to hurt someone or run off. Hurt himself. I kick Scott out of the kitchen and call my parents. They want to speak to him, but I'm not about to tell Dick I've got them on the phone. He doesn't trust anyone but me and I know I can't afford to break that trust. It's all I've got. I can hear his voice getting louder in the living room. "I need to take him somewhere," I say. "He needs help." My mother gives me the name of his old doctor; tells me where he lives. I promise to call back soon and hang up. I look the doctor's name up in the phone book and call him at home. Miraculously he answers and after just a few questions says, "Take him in a taxi to Presbyterian St Luke's Medical Center. Can you do that?"

"Yes."

"Have you got enough money?"

"I think so."

"I'll alert the hospital," he says. "OK? Can you do that now?"

I'm afraid to hang up the phone. So afraid I don't answer. The doctor says, "It'll be OK. I'll see him first thing in the morning." He pauses, then adds, "You're doing the right thing. You're a good sister."

*

I scarcely remember the taxi ride, but I think Sylvie and Scott came along. St. Luke's was on the West Side, in a bad neighborhood. I remember it was nearly midnight when we pulled into the emergency entrance. The lights were suddenly terribly bright as we stumbled out of the car, holding onto Dick's wrists and arms. I don't remember paying the taxi driver. I don't remember how or when we got back home.

My mother flew out. Dick was quickly stabilized with medication and released after just a few days. He and my mother flew home later that week, and Dick was back at Franconia for the start of the fall term.

I had two weeks left before I had to go back to Lexington and school. It all seemed so minor now, so trivial. My little life. I cleaned and saw friends and made peace with the frightened cats that didn't come out of hiding for several days. Those cats were all found abandoned as kittens in the filthy balcony of a Mexico City movie theater. They had grown fat and luxurious in the Coles' care, but their confidence was as superficial as any orphan's.

*

My mother and I patched things up in the fall. We took a Saturday morning yoga class, because I wanted to get fit and my mother was trying to learn to relax without drinking. She'd cut way back. We spent the bitter winter months planning an organic garden, poring over seed catalogues, making charts and diagrams. We calculated yields, made notes for recipes: zucchini boats and corn chowder.

In December, I'd had enough of Lexington High School and studying things that meant nothing to me. I was sixteen and knew I could legally leave school without my parents' permission. I wrote away for information on a correspondence course that would give me a high school certificate and informed my parents that I wasn't going back after

Christmas. I justified my decision to drop out again by saying I felt I was learning nothing useful there. "I've just completed nearly two years of study in one year, and I feel no more enlightened than when I started," I said. It was just like paint-by-numbers, a facts and figures education that required nothing of me. My parents didn't object. Perhaps they had run out of objections. I ordered the correspondence course and got a job as a cashier at Woolworth's in Lexington Center. I offered to pay for room and board, but my parents wouldn't accept. "Save your money," my mother said. "Without an education, you're going to need it."

In February, the girl next door invited me to a kegger. It was somebody's birthday, and I think she felt sorry for me. The evening started out tame enough, drinking beer and shooting pool in someone's basement, but then the host's parents came home, and we all piled into cars and roared off into the night. Down at the reservoir, the boys stood in a circle and smoked pot while the girls sat in cars and preened and waited. *For what?* I wondered. I got out and approached the circle. I hadn't smoked pot in months, and it smelled spicy and nice. Lights shone on the dirt track from the car park and a gold VW Sunbug slipped into the halo of lamplight where we stood. "That's Ralph Fordham," said a kid standing next to me. A tall skinny guy with impossibly long straight hair unfolded himself from the little car and walked towards the circle. Towards me.

Ralph had a motorcycle and a tough bunch of friends. He was nearly twenty, between jobs. He said he liked my long straight hair. He liked girls who wore no make-up. He was devoted to his mother and her old Irish setter. Both were infirm. The setter needed help up and down the stairs. His mother had a colostomy bag and didn't like to be seen in public. Ralph lived at home and did what he could for them. We were an item instantly.

When my mother discovered that I was riding around on Ralph's motorcycle, she took me out and bought me a leather jacket, leather pants, and a sturdy pair of boots. She invited Ralph for Sunday dinner, and asked if his spare helmet fit me properly. The following week she made an appointment for me with the clinic where she worked, and I got my first starter pack of birth control pills.

Riding on Ralph's Harley was the best thing I knew. I put up with his rough friends and their weekend-long parties, drinking beer and shooting handguns in the New Hampshire woods, in order to make the long trip back to Lexington late Sunday night with the cold biting hard and the wind tangling my hair. Coming down the mile-long grade just outside town, Ralph would wind it out to 110 mph and we would fly, the sense of speed intoxicating. I worked weekdays at Woolworth's, selling shoelaces to Mormon boys and stalking thirteen-year-old girls who shoplifted in the cosmetics aisle. I knew what to look for, and my supervisor, Blanche, praised my sharp eyes and went easy on me when it came to hard jobs like changing tubes in the long fluorescent light fixtures and hanging holiday decorations from wires strung in the ceiling. Blanche had blue hair and angry red lips and I liked her in spite of myself. I made her instant coffee with three sugars and swept the aisles with a large stiff broom at closing time. Ralph waited outside. "Tsk," said Blanche, when I slipped through the chained front door and donned my helmet. "Tsk."

*

The job at Woolworth's didn't last as long as Ralph did. A few months working retail made it abundantly clear that I should finish high school. But how? The correspondence course was worse than school. Then Ralph got a typesetting apprenticeship at a print shop and started working nights. I sat home on my hands and wondered what was next. My mother and I had planted the garden in spring and by mid-summer we were harvesting vegetables: zucchini, beans, lettuce, peas. The corn was shoulder high and the broccoli was coming on. On Sundays, we canned and froze whatever we couldn't eat or give away.

I was living in two worlds: the late-night boozy world of Ralph and his biker friends and the daytime world of weeding and harvesting and simple, mind-numbing work. I read an item in the local paper about a student art show at the Cambridge School of Weston, a private high school not too far from where I lived. "Small, progressive, offering an array of college-like studies. Students free to choose their own courses. Weaving, pottery, dance. Outdoor education." I called and requested a brochure. The woman on the phone asked if I would also like an application. "Yes," I found myself saying. "Yes, please."

*

I spent one happy academic year at The Cambridge School, studying Russian History through Art, Music, and Literature; and Earth Science and the Ecology Movement. I wrote an essay about the role of imagination in critical thinking and was excused from the standard second-year algebra requirement. I took pottery and weaving classes and spent a month hiking and climbing in the Asheville Gorge wilderness on an Outward Bound trek. I paid half the tuition with my Woolworth's savings. My Grampa Down chipped in the other half.

Throughout the year, I continued to see Ralph. Most

afternoons, when he wasn't working, Ralph picked me up from school. He had traded in his VW bug for a vintage '56 Cadillac hearse, and we would cruise around pretending we were Bud Cort and Ruth Gordon in a scene from *Harold and Maude*.

The Cambridge School was miles away from home and nowhere near a bus route. When Ralph was working, I had to hang around after school and wait for my mother to swing by on her way home from work. About half the students boarded at school, so there was always something going on in the afternoons. I spent a lot of time in the art studio where I met Mary from Michigan and Sasha from Maine. Mary and Sasha were roommates. They lived in a little cabin in the woods behind the main dorm. Soon I was a regular visitor to the cabin, where we spent long afternoons listening to music and talking politics and spirituality and whatever else came to mind.

As the year progressed, I began to feel resentful of Ralph. When he picked me up from school, I was sulky and quick to find fault. I picked little fights on the way home. It never occurred to me to invite him to stay on campus and hang out with my friends. He was older, for one thing, and rough around the edges. Working class. It was a difference I was ashamed to admit. My fellow students came from wealthy families. They were well-educated, worldly, politically aware—all the things I'd loved about my Evanston friends. All the things Ralph was not.

Towards the end of the year, I started applying to colleges and universities. My top choice was Hampshire, which was only a couple of hours away. But I also applied to Evergreen in Washington State, where my brother had recently transferred, and to Goddard in Northern Vermont. Ralph was increasingly sullen and withdrawn. He was worried about being left behind, but I found I cared less and less. I hung on for a while out of loyalty and obligation. But I was less interested in the weekend drinking parties, riding around in cars and the heavy metal music his friends preferred.

Shortly before graduation, I resolved to break up with Ralph. I'd decided to spend the summer at home. My art teacher, Randy, had offered me a part-time weaving apprenticeship for two months. I'd get to learn about production weaving, helping him prepare scarves and shawls for the Rhinebeck Craft Fair in October. I'd get to help my mother with the garden. We'd expanded this year to a 20'x30' plot on my grandparents' land in Pepperell. I'd been accepted to Hampshire, and I was starting in the fall.

On graduation weekend, Ralph picked me up in the hearse and I told him we needed to talk. He drove to an isolated spot near a pond in the woods and I said it as simply as I could: "I don't want to go out with you anymore" and "I'm sorry" and "I wish I could feel differently than I do, but I'm changing and my life is changing and it's what I have to do" and "I'm sorry."

Ralph might've gotten angry, he might've thrown something and broken it or even hit me. He didn't. He broke down and sobbed. Huge, heaving sobs. And by the end of the afternoon, I was consoling him in the back of the hearse. It was the most wooden sex we'd ever had, and it didn't help matters at all.

I didn't see Ralph again after that, but the following month I missed my period. I'd been feeling tired and queasy and I'd missed a couple of days of work. Randy was irritated with me, and the garden was overrun with weeds. I was pregnant.

My mother arranged everything. She took me to the clinic and my urine sample tested positive. She sat quietly in the room as I talked with the counsellor. "Yes, I was using birth control." "I'm on the pill, but sometimes I forget to take it." "No, I don't want to have a baby." "I'm going to college in the fall." "Yes, I want an abortion." I had to say all of those things, especially the last one.

That same afternoon, my mother made an appointment for me with one of the clinic's doctors, a woman. "She's very good, Abby," my mother said. "It will hurt. You'll probably feel sick afterwards. There'll be some cramping, maybe some bleeding. It'll be alright."

The following Thursday, my mother and I drove to the clinic where she worked. She walked me in, announced my arrival. Sat with me and smoothed the hair from my face. After the procedure, when I was resting in the recovery room, she brought in a cool cloth and washed my face. Then she sat beside the bed and held my hand while I slept a little.

Six weeks later, I left home for good.

Disclosures

My brother has bipolar disorder. The illness was not correctly diagnosed until after his third hospitalization in November 1978. The diagnosing psychiatrist, Jean Campbell, was Scottish-trained and had a different perspective from most American psychiatrists at that time. Prior to Jean Campbell's diagnosis, it was assumed he suffered from paranoid schizophrenia. Intense manic periods and delusions associated with his early episodes were invariably brought on by drug use, prescription or otherwise. He writes:

> I felt a lot of depression in the summer of 1971 and feelings of isolation. In mid-August I had my wisdom teeth out and the dentist gave me a large dose of cortisone steroids to take over a ten-day period, to prevent swelling. We went to Sioux City where I started to feel sick. Grampa Down gave me Valium. We came home (me still taking the steroids). I got more agitated, and the jump ensued.

With characteristic generosity, my brother goes on to explain that the only times he was hospitalized as an adult (in 1985 and 1987), the manic episodes were caused by his own recklessness. He'd been prescribed lithium for his bipolar condition but was not taking it.

*

In the early 1990s, my mother began having trouble with figures and sums. She suffered spells of vertigo, moments of static confusion. The distance from the edge of the car to the edge of the road was blurring, and her reactions while driving were noticeably slower. She took herself off the road, preferring a circuitous commute by bus to the hazards of the wheel.

My mother bought a secondary level math workbook and painstakingly completed all the pages. She was trying to work out what was happening to her, how much damage had already occurred. She began to leave unfinished crossword puzzles in little piles around the house. Recipes were increasingly difficult to follow.

"The first signs of the family illness," my brother whispered in a furtive phone call during an unnerving visit he was having with my parents. No one wanted to believe that she had been struck, but the signs were mounting.

My mother's co-workers at the campus bookstore began to notice gaps in her performance: she was having trouble transcribing book numbers onto order forms and shelving books in proper order. In the spring of 1992, after a poor performance review, she reluctantly took medical leave. In private, she began researching options for long-term care. She was sixty-two.

Worry increased with forgetfulness. My mother kept elaborate lists on which she mapped the events of each day in minute detail. Planning became an obsession, a way to hold on. By autumn, her own home had become a complex and occasionally unfathomable terrain; she was terrified that she wouldn't be able to navigate the route from living room to bathroom when the need arose. Unsteady on her feet, she began to need guidance when walking outdoors.

I was married in 1994. Joe and I held the wedding in San Francisco, our chosen city, where we'd been living for a couple of years. My in-laws-to-be, who didn't fly in airplanes, came all the way out from Pittsburgh on a Greyhound bus. My parents also attended although my mother was having greater difficulty walking. Her steps, short and uncertain, her hands held stiffly in the air in front of her. The photos from that weekend betray the rigidity of her posture; her features clouded with anxiety and strain. This would be one of her last trips, though we didn't know it at the time. She and my father still talked of the European vacation they'd always meant to take.

It wasn't long before my mother needed help to lift her body from a chair and assistance at the toilet. A full-time caregiver was engaged. Then came the night when my mother fell on the stairs and my father couldn't lift her. They stayed there, prone and uncomfortable—my father holding my mother's hand while he wedged her in place with the weight of his body to keep her from slipping—and waited for the caregiver to arrive at 8 a.m.

Of the many symptoms that characterized the progression of my mother's illness, one stands out as particularly cruel. During her last few years, she had difficulty initiating movement. Imagine having the desire to reach for something coveted—a cherished photograph or a ripe peach—but lacking the ability to engage the muscles that lift your hand. Simple tasks such as turning the pages of a book were now impossible. Her speech was increasingly inhibited, too.

The night before Sofia was born, my mother used the telephone for the first time in over a year. No one would've thought her able to direct her fingers on the keypad, let alone remember the sequence of numbers that dialed home and woke my father. She had a burning question and it couldn't wait.

2 a.m. My father was shaken from a solid sleep by the ring of the phone. He feared the worst. Had she fallen? Choked? Just recently, the neurologist had explained the probable cause of my mother's death would be self-asphyxiation. She'd no longer be able to move the muscles of her throat and, unable to swallow or to clear it, she would drown in a tiny pool of her own saliva.

The voice on the other end of the line was husky, quietly determined: "Have you heard anything from San Francisco?" my mother asked.

*

My mother was sixty-nine when she died of a compound neurological disorder. As specified in her will, a complete autopsy with extensive brain tissue analysis was performed. Her cremated remains were not available for burial until nearly five months after her death. A copy of the diagnosis arrived in a manila envelope later that year: Dementia with Lewy Bodies, a kind of plaque, which attaches itself to the brain tissue and causes a slow and irreversible atrophying of the tissue and related neurophysiologic functions.

The family illness.

*

At the graveside service, my cousins spontaneously sing the old cowboy lullaby, "Desert Silvery Blue." Even little Sofia knows the words to Grammy Ivanie's song.

Erich talks lovingly of all the attention my mother paid him as a young child, about how present she was in his life. All my cousins nod their heads. A few of them wipe their eyes. Alex says, "She taught us all those songs, those old camp songs. She even made us little books with the lyrics so that we'd remember."

I stood there in shock, feeling a little sick in the buzzing August heat. Little books? She never made me a little book. Where was I when she was lovingly attending my cousins?

Where was I?

*

It's late winter, 1999. I'm sitting in my mother's room at Montclair. Patchy remnants of ice molder on the wheat-colored lawn and a steel grey sky presses down on the horizon. I'm restlessly scanning the bleak landscape when a bright red ribbon streaks past the window. "Look!" I say, pointing just outside where seed is scattered below a feeder. "A cardinal—just there." My mother turns her head stiffly, mouth open and crusty at the edges. "He's alone," she grimaces and leans stiffly towards the window. "He's wearing his red jacket. Maybe—he doesn't have a mate—or maybe he's an assistant." She pauses for a moment. "Too many males—or is it not enough females?" There is another long pause, and then she lifts her fingers from her lap and flexes them into stiff points. Her thick nails are carefully shaped and varnished an icy pink. At Montclair, manicures are part of the social program. My mother no longer objects and they've long since lost the entrance notes in which she indicated no interest in such things. She says, "Cardinals mate for life. I don't know what provisions they have if one dies. Maybe another takes his place."

This is the longest continuous speech my mother has managed in months. Her entire body has gone rigid with the effort of concentration. "A lot has been discussed about

119

the psychology of birds," she continues, "but not here, not in this place." There is urgency in her voice. She turns and searches my face as if she's misplaced something there. I want to grab the handles of her chair and wheel her right out of this end-of-the-road place. I try to relax, look happy, but my mother fells me with one last declaration: "No science of any kind."

Epilogue

Winter in Wellington, and the buds are popping out rashly on flowering bushes and trees. It's the first sign of the season turning. During the one warm week that always comes with the return of early morning light, Sofia announces that she wants to plant a garden. It's too soon, I warn her, and, besides, we have no yard. Our house clings to a bushy precipice that rises abruptly from the road. All we have are a deck and the prevailing winds. But she insists. OK," I say, "we'll buy pots and soil and bulbs," but I don't feel hopeful.

A week later, the first shoots appear, pale green and impossibly tender. I begin to worry about the wind. At five weeks, the pots are crowded with shoots and we have to pull some to make room for others to grow. It's hard to choose and Sofia feels sad all afternoon. She wants to know what happens to things when they die. She asks me, "Where did Grammy Ivanie go?"

Winter slams back in and today is the coldest day of the year. Out in our garden, a miniature grape hyacinth has parted the soil to reveal a sturdy cup of leaves. In its center, an unlikely purple cluster pushes upwards towards the light.

*

The first things I notice are the bookshelves. They're empty.

Sofia and I have come to Omaha to visit my father. Although we've seen him a few times since we moved to New Zealand, we haven't come home since my mother died. I've come here as much to check up on my dad as to give Sofia a chance to spend time with him. I want a warm holiday in the midst of the Southern Hemisphere winter. I want to comb through boxes of family memorabilia and photographs. And I want to talk to my brother, my father, and my aunt.

The house has an eerie, unused look. Abandoned, as if the inhabitants have simply vanished. Tell-tale layers of dust gather on surfaces. Thick cobwebs climb between the stereo cabinet and speakers. Even the tiny guest towels in the downstairs bathroom have acquired a layer of fine grey dust like a powdering of snow. Everything is as orderly as I would expect—my father is fastidious—but there's something else. This house doesn't feel lived in at all.

As soon as we settle in, things begin to break. My dad tells us not to turn on the downstairs bathroom taps: they're stuck with disuse. This makes sense, of course. My dad tries not to use this bathroom, so he won't have to clean it. It's a big house, after all. Why should he make extra work for himself? Then, on the second day, the upstairs toilet quits, the line to its bulb rusted through. The kitchen faucet suddenly stops giving water. When I try to dry a load of clothes, I discover that the heating element in the dryer has blown.

The centerpiece of every room in this house has always been a bookshelf, filled to capacity or overflowing. On his last visit, my brother painstakingly categorized all of them—biography, history, fiction, poetry, art—hundreds of books, maybe thousands, and then he alphabetized each category by author or title. It took him days.

Now the shelves in every room have been swept clear of all but a half-dozen or so titles each. Up in the spare bedroom the two hand-carved bookshelves from Sioux City are empty but for a few curious titles: an Audubon survey of North American wild birds, and a collection of girl's readers from the 1930s. Gone are all the lovely little hardcover novels, *Black Beauty* and the others. Her novels, the ones my mother read and re-read as a girl.

On the afternoon of the second day, before my brother and my aunt arrive, I ask my dad, "What happened to all the books?"

"I sold them."

*

Every family has secrets and deceptions, unspoken rules about what can and can't be told. About when the truth is permissible, and when lies are required. Another daughter might press the point. She might, for instance, ask her father, "Why?" I let it go and take Sofia out in the yard to toss a ball around until the sun goes down and the fireflies come winking out of the grass.

*

Things add up. My father never answers the phone when it rings but waits to see if the caller will leave a message. He tells us he gets far too many telemarketers, and it's easier just to screen the calls. My brother, who now prefers to be called Richard, and I run out for some milk, and as soon as we're away from the house, my brother expresses concern. "This business of screening the calls: it's a helluva way to run a home office," he says. Post-retirement, my father has become a personal financial planner to make ends meet. He helps people figure out how to invest and save for their retirement. He has dozens of casual clients and is paid entirely by commission. He uses his home phone as his primary business line. He ought to answer it whenever he can.

"We can put him on that national list to block telemarketing calls," Richard says. "That'd help, but I think maybe it's his hearing. We should maybe think about helping him get a hearing aid."

"Yeah, maybe," I say, trying not to sound too unenthusiastic. My dad's not avoiding telemarketers. He's avoiding creditors. He's in deep shit, and he's not telling the truth, probably not even to himself.

The following day, my aunt Karen and I make a run to the supermarket for a chicken. We're going to make a meal at home, and Karen's buying the wine. There are so many things I want to ask her, but I'm having trouble getting started.

"So, how do you think my dad's doing?"

"He seems good, his health is good," she hedges. We chat a little about all the things that are breaking down around the house, about how difficult it is for him to keep up such a big place on his own. It isn't long before Karen's telling me about the twenty thousand dollars my dad borrowed from them a couple of years ago.

"It's not the money," Karen says. I sense she's been looking for an opportunity to mention this to me, and that she's choosing her words very carefully. This is something she does well, a quality I used to distrust. I grew up preferring what I saw as my mother's considerably more candid, less guarded nature. Now I'm not so sure who is the more honest one. I look at my aunt's face; from the side, with her straight, blunt-cut silver hair and her chiselled, high cheekbones, Karen and my mother look so alike. For the umpteenth time since Karen arrived two days ago, I check myself for the urge to listen for my mother's voice in her words.

"It's really not a matter of the money," Karen repeats. "That's something I wanted to do for my sister." She means,

126

help with the nursing home costs. "At the time, when he asked us for it, we tried to give it as a gift—our contribution—but your dad insisted it was to be a loan, temporary. He insisted on paying it back." My aunt stops, then starts again, a little uncomfortably. "That was more than two years ago. He's never mentioned it to us again."

*

Deceptions mount. The visit is fraught with them. We're sitting together in the living room on Karen's last day with us. Sofia has just given us a little concert on her violin. Richard lifts his head and gazes myopically around the room. "Jesus, Dad," as if he's just noticed, "where are all the books?"

"Oh, they'll be back," my dad says, cryptically.

"Yeah, but where are they?"

"They're on loan," my dad says, as if he's practiced it in front of the mirror. "On loan—to the church."

My brother is skeptical, and he groans about all the work he did, less than a year ago, organizing all the books. My aunt is busying herself with a drawing of Sofia's she's picked up from the coffee table. She's completely detached from the conversation, which is dripping with falsity. Not one of us, I suspect, believes what's being said, but no one admits it. It's a round robin of saving face.

Incredibly, I find myself trying to cover for my dad. "You mean like a lending program?" I say, brightly.

My dad either doesn't hear me, or he's too afraid to stray from the script. "Don't you worry," he says, and then he repeats, "they'll be back."

*

127

I'm used to the stuff around money. That's been going on for a long time. But it's gotten noticeably worse. We go out to dinner one night with a group of my dad's friends, and on the way, he asks me if I can loan him cash to pay for the meal. "We invited everyone," he says, "so it should be our treat." I tell him I'll just put it on my credit card, which I do, but he insists on giving me a check for $237 to cover the bill. It's as if the act of insisting he's going to pay it back relieves him of the burden of humility. He hands me the check, all smiles. He's paid for dinner.

When I get back to New Zealand a couple of days later, I have an email waiting for me. I knew I would. "Abby," it says. "Will you do me a favor and HOLD the $237 check for a few days. I will let you know as soon as I think that it's OK to deposit it." He goes on to mention all the unexpected expenses he's been hit with, such as plumbing bills and the dryer repair. I've lost count of the small and large loans I've made these past several years, all to be paid back just as soon as next month's commission check comes in. Dignity has a high price. I'm beginning to think it's claimed my dad's sanity.

"No worries," I write back. "I've ripped up the check. Dinner's on us."

*

The way I remember it, my mother stopped driving before she stopped working; I remember talking with her about commuting by bus. I've tried and failed and tried again to capture the early impact of the disease on my mother's physical and mental health in poetry, in essays, and even in the eulogy I wrote for her memorial service. I thought I'd finally captured something of its indiscriminate cruelty, the desperate losses suffered as her brain began to atrophy and her faculties to shut down one by one by one, in metaphors of navigation: preferring a circuitous route by bus to the hazards of the road.

A few days before travelling to Omaha, while talking with my dad on the phone, he tells me that my mother didn't stop driving until her very last day of work; this casual pronouncement suddenly renders the text and my memory inaccurate, fallible. In a panic, I start checking all sorts of critical facts. It's possible that while I've been relying so heavily on my own memories, I've mixed up entirely too much. It's possible that the story I've told is all wrong.

*

My aunt and I are standing at the counter in the kitchen, chopping vegetables and sipping wine. I tell her about this dilemma, about not being sure whose story I'm writing, whose truth I'm telling. As an example, I tell her what my dad remembers about my mother giving up her car. Then I tell her how I wrote it. Karen listens quietly, thoughtfully. When I'm done, she cocks her head. "You know, Abby," she says, "I remember it the way you do."

I press a little harder. "What else do you remember?"

My aunt sighs, almost imperceptibly. "Well," she pauses. "There were things—there were just some things that Ivanie and I never discussed. There were some things we never said."

A door swings shut, and I don't knock again. Another niece might say: "What things? Since when?" But silence is all I can muster.

This is how my dad tells the story:

"I remember it clearly, like it was just yesterday." My dad is standing on the opposite side of the kitchen counter. He's just come in from collecting the day's mail. I'm drying dishes and putting them away.

"Earlier that spring, she'd had a poor performance review from her boss at Creighton." My mother worked at the University bookstore, where she was the medical textbook buyer. She had been struggling for some time with basic tasks such as running the cash register and shelving books. Shortly after the performance review she decided to go on disability. She'd been looking into it for some time. When she told her boss, he convinced her to stay on an extra two weeks to help get them through the big spring inventory. "Ivanie was still driving every day," my dad says.

When he gets going, my dad comes alive. He recounts anecdotes at great length, sparing no detail. His voice takes on an oratory tone and his eyes grow moist and seem to sparkle. He calls her "Ivanie," not "your mother;" it's as if I've faded from view and he's been transported back to the moment, to the place he'd rather dwell.

"The morning of her last day, her co-workers gave a breakfast in her honor at a café not far from the university. After breakfast, when Ivanie left the café to drive to work, she became disoriented. She wasn't familiar with the route and she suddenly had to cross two lanes of traffic to make a left turn. Maybe she just couldn't judge the distance, but she sideswiped a pick-up truck. No one was hurt. There was damage to both vehicles, but she could still drive the car. After exchanging information with the other driver, Ivanie drove to the bookstore, parked her car and worked a full day. She never said a thing to anyone."

The depth of my father's admiration is palpable, as if that kind of stoicism, that bravery in the face of adversity is the most admirable quality he can imagine.

"She drove the car home that night," my father continues, "parked in the garage and came into the house. She threw her keys down here on the counter." I can imagine the wry twist of her mouth as she tossed the keys. "'That's it,' she'd said. 'I'm through with driving.'"

*

Back in Wellington, I'm cooking breakfast when the phone rings. It's my dad. I speak with him briefly and hand the phone to Sofia so I can get back to the eggs. She chats happily for several minutes and when I put the food on the table, I ask Sofia to say goodbye.

The following morning when Sofia's at school, my dad calls again. He's bursting to tell me about their conversation.

"I asked Sofia if she knew what day it was," my dad reports. "'No, Grampie,' Sofia replied. 'What day is it?'"

"It's Father's Day."

"Oh!"

"Don't you have anything you'd like to say to me?"

"Like what, Grampie?"

"Well, like 'Happy Father's Day, Grampie!'"

"Then," my dad says, "there was a long pause and finally Sofia said, 'Don't you have a daughter for that?'"

My dad's chuckling merrily. He says, "Does that remind you of anyone, Abby?"

I'm laughing too, but I've got a fist around my heart. I know exactly what he means. *Ivanie's sense of humor.*

It's exactly what my mother would have said.

*

My parents met on a blind date and didn't exactly get along. My mother was, perhaps, a little superior. My father was trying hard, though not necessarily with her. They argued about politics, although, in truth, they agreed on most things.

A year later, my father was home for the holidays and wanted a date to go dancing. He thought of my mother but couldn't remember her name. He started calling the dorms at Wellesley, and when someone answered he asked, "Is there a girl there with an unusual name?" On the third try, the person who answered said, "Oh, you mean Ivanie!" and my mother was called to the phone.

It's an old story.

My parents graduated in 1953 and went to live on an Army base, while my father served his time. After he was discharged, my father went back to Dartmouth and got an MBA. My mother gave up the idea of medical school and worked part-time in a pathology lab. They had two children, a boy first and then a girl—my brother and me—the children my mother had always wanted. She cooked and cleaned and baked and made Halloween costumes. She read to us, sang to us and held us when we cried. She set aside her own ambitions and her considerable intellect went largely unnoticed.

She loved us, even when she herself felt unlovable. Of this I'm sure.

Acknowledgements

This memoir was written in fulfillment of a Master of Arts in Creative Writing at the International Institute of Modern Letters, Victoria University of Wellington, in 2004. I am indebted to my classmates and to Damien Wilkins who convened our course. I owe a particular debt of gratitude to my MA supervisor, Professor Harry Ricketts who offered coffee, close reading and insightful criticism and always made me feel worthy of the task.

To all my teachers—Judith Barrington, Lucinda Roy, Dinah Hawken, Shannon Welch, Harry Ricketts, Mark Doty, Damien Wilkins, Eirlys Hunter and Anna Blake—thank you.

To the writers who have offered unparalleled support and astute criticism over the years—in particular, Lewis Buzbee and Sabrina Malcolm—thank you.

And thanks, too, to my husband, Joe Letteri, and daughter, Sofia Letteri, for the gifts of time and love.

The completion and publication of this memoir would not have been possible without my brother, Richard Joslin, whose passionate support of *down they forgot* is truly exceptional. I am grateful for his unfailing generosity, and for his wit and keen memory.

@abbyletteri.bsky.social